JERSEY RAMBLES

Cover: *Hazel and Susie Jones on the coast path from Fliquet to St. Catherine's; see Walk 7*

*Le Moulin de Quetivel, showing course of the mill stream which
powered the overshot waterwheel downstream: Walk 18*

JERSEY RAMBLES

~ Coast and Country ~

John Le Dain

Illustrations by Edward Dowden

SEAFLOWER BOOKS

First published in 1992
Revised edition 1997;
Reprinted 1998, 2001 and 2003 with further revisions
by SEAFLOWER BOOKS

Seaflower Books is an imprint of
Ex Libris Press, to whom all enquiries
and correspondence should be addressed:

EX LIBRIS PRESS
1 The Shambles
Bradford on Avon
Wiltshire
BA15 1JS

Typeset in 10 point Palatino

Design and Typesetting by Ex Libris Press
Cover printed by Shires Press, Trowbridge
Printed and bound in Britain by
Cromwell Press, Trowbridge, Wiltshire

The maps in this book, other than that on pages 8/9, are reproduced
with the permission of the Island Development Committee and
based upon the 1988 1:25,000 scale map prepared by
Ordnance Survey for the Island Development Committee.
Crown/ IDC copyright reserved

ISBN 0 948578 37 8

To the memory of my Jersey mother, Gladys Jones, née Le Dain

Contents

'But, reader, if you can, walk, and so add tenfold to your pleasure; for many of the most beautiful places in the island are usually unvisited by strangers, owing to the lazy habit of indulging only in carriage exercise. Drive if you like (and indeed ladies must do so) to some inn in the vicinity of the scene you intend visiting; but when you have put up your carriage start for a walk, as far as your strength will allow you.'

A passage from the book *The Channel Islands: Pictorial, Legendary, and Descriptive*, by Octavius Rooke, published in 1856, and as true today as it was then (apart from the bit about ladies!)

Introduction

Jersey conjures up a mixed image in many people's minds. Famous for its cows and early potatoes, its golden beaches and generous sunshine, it is also known world-wide as an offshore tax haven and, as such, does not always invite uncritical comment.

Jersey is perhaps not a priority destination for those holiday-makers with a penchant for rambling, yet to miss the opportunity of walking at least a portion of the island's network of footpaths and lanes is to miss the real charm of Jersey – the attractions of its countryside and less frequented coastal stretches. In particular, the almost continual footpath along the north coast gives access to some of the most spectacular coastal scenery in the whole of the British Isles.

Footpaths inland are not as widespread as they are on the mainland, though a few do exist and many short stretches have been opened of late. Rights of way which cross private property, in particular fields and woods, to which one is accustomed in England, are pretty much the exception. In compensation there exists an intricate network of little used country lanes, many of which have been designated 'Green Lanes' in recent years, with priority given to walkers, riders and cyclists.

Jersey is a most beautiful island. I have been visiting every year since 1945 and, on every visit, I am surprised and delighted by its sheer attractiveness. The island is a gem – shaped roughly as a rectangle nine miles by five (45 square miles in all), its bold outline encompasses an incredible variety of scenery. Jersey is essentially a platform rising out of the sea and tilted southwards (thus making the most of its sheltered position in the Bay of Mont St. Michel) with a number of valleys draining north-south. The north coast is craggy and defiant, the south gentle and lush, the west wild and windswept, the east pastoral and intimate. A favourite question posed by locals is, 'Which side of the island do you like best?' I always find it

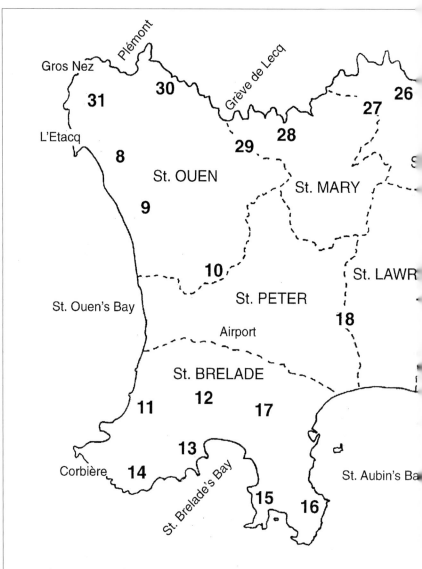

Outline map of Jersey, showing the twelve parishes and the main points around the coast.
The numbers refer to the approximate whereabouts of each of the 31 walks described in this book.

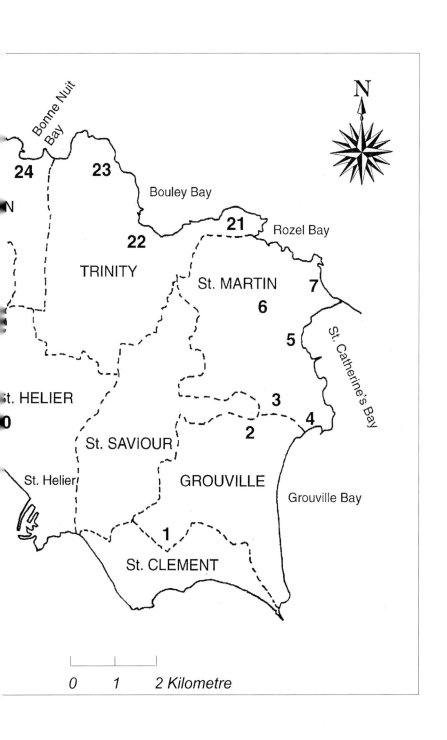

N

Bonne Nuit Bay

24   23

Bouley Bay

22   21   Rozel Bay

TRINITY

St. MARTIN   7

6

5

St. Catherine's Bay

St. HELIER

0   3

2   4

St. SAVIOUR

St. Helier

GROUVILLE

Grouville Bay

1

St. CLEMENT

0   1   2 Kilometre

impossible to answer this question if choosing one side in particular means rejecting the other three.

Few places on Earth can be as intensively farmed as Jersey. There are fields which slope at incredibly steep angles (known locally as côtils) so that one wonders how the farmer can sow his seed and harvest his crop. Certainly such difficult terrain is rarely cultivated on the mainland.

Happily, the farmers have left the very steepest valley sides to woodland. Many of the main roads which penetrate inland from the south coast naturally follow valleys, which are generally well wooded, so that you get the impression that Jersey supports more trees than it actually does.

Much of the landscape is a patchwork of hedged fields, tiny in comparison to England and France, but all productive of grass for the famous cattle, or of a range of vegetables and flowers, a range which seems to include ever more exotic species as each year passes. These high value crops in tiny fields demand a good deal of handwork and it is a pleasurable surprise to see people working on the land with nothing more than a hoe and a fork and painfully bent back.

Given its modest dimensions, Jersey is densely populated, yet the Island remains remarkably unspoilt and, St. Helier aside, you would never guess what a huge population this small island now supports. Comparative prosperity means that properties are well maintained, though it is always good to see an old Jersey stone house with its original sash windows, perhaps painted a serviceable green, instead of repointed granite featuring unnaturally white PVC double glazed units.

Statistics indicate that Jersey has the highest number of cars per head in the world – higher even than the USA and twice as many as the mainland. I rest my case. I always sing the praises of the Jersey bus service – a comprehensive network of routes, buses manned by (usually) cheerful driver/conductors, and a regular, reliable service. If only the authorities would market the service more forcefully perhaps fewer holidaymakers would feel it necessary to add to the road congestion by hiring cars. Out of town car parking facilities are detailed in this book but so too are bus routes – a bus ride is a much more relaxing and hassle-free way to begin or end a ramble!

The routes recommended in this book are a selection of the best walks available on the island. They vary considerably in length and can be adapted in an infinite variety of ways. The essential companion to this book is the 1:25,000 Ordnance Survey map of Jersey which is remarkably cheap and details every field boundary, house and lane on this Island. If you are not using a car, your other essential companion is a bus timetable, also inexpensive and very clear, and obtainable from the bus office at the Weighbridge.

I have tried to be as helpful as possible in describing these rambles and in the information I have set down. Details of the walks and how to reach the starting points are given at the outset of each walk. These are followed by detailed directions in which any visible sign is highlighted in the text in bold type. Finally, brief explanations of particular points of interest featured during the walks are offered.

However you get there and back, once you begin walking you are guaranteed to see Jersey at its very best!

John Le Dain
Le Bolthole, St. Helier

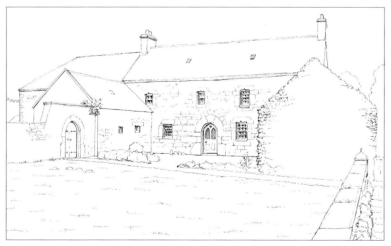

An old Jersey house, Leoville Farm, St. Ouen

Jersey National Trust sign, Mont Ubé

GROUVILLE CIRCULAR

*Grouville Village via Le Croix de la Bataille, Mont Ubé
and St Clement's Church*

This undemanding walk is mainly along quiet, pleasant lanes offering some good views around an unfrequented corner of the island. There is a shop in Grouville village and a pub just over half way on the main road east of St. Clement's Church.

Start:	Grouviille village centre
Map Reference:	O.S. 692485
Bus:	1B to Grouville Church
Parking:	A short distance along the main road uphill from Grouville Church and village centre, on the right opposite the Parish Room.
Distance:	5 kilometres

With your back to the entrance gate to **Grouville Church**, turn right and walk up the main road to the rather austere looking Parish Room, where you take the minor lane just to its left. Follow the lane uphill until you see the cross marking St. Joseph's R.C. Church. The lane begins to level out just as you reach the road junction, distinguished by a grassy triangle which supports half a dozen trees and a stone-capped well. This spot is known as **Le Jardin de la Croix de la Bataille** and belongs to the Jersey National Trust.

Carry on to join the main road, the A3 to St. Helier, beside which, thankfully, there is a pavement. At the point where there is a sharp right-hand bend you continue straight ahead by a lane.

After a short distance a wide view opens up on your right, in a westerly direction, across the flat unbuilt expanse of Samares towards St. Helier and across St. Aubin's Bay towards Noirmont. The lane becomes deeply incised as it descends. Carry on until you reach a T-junction where you turn left. Straight ahead you can see the bosky slopes of Mont Ubé. The lane bears right just before **Mont Ubé House**. A few yards further, opposite the red brick house, notice a stone in the wall on the left inscribed '**Dolmen de Mont Ubé, Société Jersiaise**'.

Climb the steps and follow the path which ascends the wooded slope to reach the dolmen which is very impressive in its proportions, its completeness, and its peaceful, secret setting. Across the field, beyond the dolmen, you can see the curious Nicolle Tower.

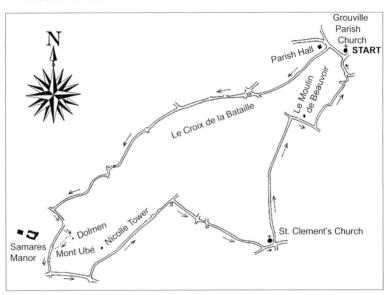

Leaving the dolmen you bear left along the beaten path and through the woods until you eventually reach the lane above **Samares Manor** where you can see the quadrangle of farm buildings attached to the Manor, which is itself situated just beyond. Bear left past **La Blinerie** (the lane has the same name) to reach the main road where you turn left, in an easterly direction.

Follow the pavement on the far side. You can see Nicolle Tower at the top of the sloping field opposite. Take the first turning on the left. Continue along this lane, ascending steadily with widening views east across the low-lying and vulnerable south-east corner of the island, thickly defended against invasion from France by a number of Martello towers.

Just past the **Garden Centre** you will meet the opening of **Rue de Genestet** on your right. Do not take this lane but, instead, make for the narrow metalled path immediately to its left. This is a charming, sunken way which forms a boundary between fields on either side. Follow the path which leads directly to **St. Clement's Church**, passing the parish's Millennium standing stone en route.

Leave the churchyard by the steps on the far side which drop you on to **Rue Laurens** where you turn left. In spring there is a vigorous growth of stinking onions, with their delicate, white, bluebell-like flowers, on the far bank here. Climb up the sunken lane until you reach a T-junction with the unmistakable mass of a former windmill, now without its sails, on your right. Turn right here and walk past **Le Moulin de Beauvoir**, and then left down a very narrow lane from which you can see the tip of Grouville Church spire ahead. This is a splendid finale to the walk with, on a clear day, tremendous views to the right across Grouville Bay to Gorey Castle and the coast of France at the horizon. When you reach the main road below bear left to reach the church/ village store/ car park/ bus stop.

Grouville Church

Very much the focal point of Grouville village, the Church of St. Martin's of Grouville, with its tall white, plastered spire, occupies a corner site beside the main island route which links St. Helier with Gorey. It is well worth entering this church, with its nave, chancel with two adjoining chapels and its medieval relics, notably the font (which has a long and chequered past), the piscinas and a recess in the south chapel containing a mysterious carved head with a hole in the middle of its forehead.

Le Jardin de la Croix de la Bataille

This fragment of land, which forms a green triangle isolated by three roads, is the property of the Jersey National Trust which has erected a traditional Jersey well-head over the deep well situated here. The battle referred to was fought in 1406 against an invading army of about a thousand, mainly French and Spanish. The lane from here to Grouville Church was known as Blood Hill in remembrance of those who fell and were carted off for a Christian burial.

Samares Manor

The name 'samares' is a corruption of *salse marais* (= salt-water marsh) and comprises an area of low-lying land in St. Clement's Parish where sea water was allowed to evaporate leaving salt. Samares Manor has a history dating back to early Norman times, though it has changed hands often. All that remains from that period is the remarkable crypt of the Manorial chapel, but the house we see today is surely one of the most charming and unusual in the island. It is open to the public and is worth a visit. The grounds, complete with *colombier*, or dovecote, are a delight, whilst the herb garden is sublime. It is possible to join a guided tour of the house; you may also explore the adjacent quadrangle of farm buildings with its menagerie of domestic animals.

The Dolmen at Mont Ubé

Mont Ubé

Now the property of La Société Jersiaise (the local antiquarian society which has a hand in the island's museums) is a dolmen, or burial chamber, dating from about 2,000 B.C. In the early nineteenth century it was used as a pigsty and later in the century its capstones were taken for building material. Its 28 upright stones remain to form a passage leading to the burial-chamber which had three side chambers. Originally the whole structure would have been covered with earth, like the great dolmen at Hougue Bie.

Lane above Gorey

GOREY VILLAGE CIRCULAR

Gorey Village via Queen's Valley Reservoir

This is a pleasant, short walk which introduces Gorey, a location with a genuine village atmosphere, and the varied countryside which backs on to it.

Start:	Gorey Village Centre
Map Reference:	706498
Bus:	No. 1 to Gorey; ask for Gorey Village
Parking:	On the left of the main road to Gorey, signposted 'To Gorey village and Shops'
Distance:	4 kilometres

From the coast road, take the road leading inland and signposted '**To Gorey Village Shops**'. You will see 'The Secret Garden' Tea Rooms and garden on your left and the tower and spire of Gorey Church on the hill-top to your right.

Turn right past **Rosedale Stores** and the Catholic Church. Take the left fork and begin a gentle ascent. Further uphill you take a left fork once more. Now, from this height, you have great views over Gorey Village and harbour and the majestic proportions of the mighty castle. The wide expanse of Grouville Bay is defined to the south by La Rocque, Jersey's most south-easterly point and, more than a mile offshore, by Seymour Tower. There is much recent development in Gorey Village, with many new houses on the landward side of the old village core.

At the summit of the next rise once again take the left-hand fork, then left at the next T-junction. From this ridge-top lane you can see across Queen's Valley to your right and down towards

Grouville to your left.

As the way bends left to meet another lane you can turn right to reach Grouville Village and left to return to Gorey. If you turn left you simply follow this quiet 'back' lane – to your left are the wooded slopes which shut off Queen's Valley to the north whilst on the right are the flat lands of Les Marais which enclose Les Maltières, a wetland habitat recognisable from this slightly elevated lane by a vigorous growth of crack willow and other moisture-loving plants. This constitutes an important staging post for migrant birds and is maintained by the Jersey National Trust.

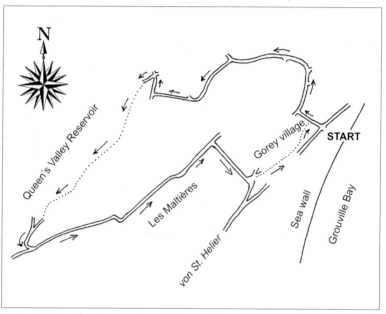

Just after the iron gates of **Gorey House** to your left turn right along the road in a seaward direction. Before you reach the main road, bear left to follow the pleasant path which follows the edge of the green beside the stream which drains Les Marais. This is a lovely meadow, and sometimes a number of tethered Jersey cows can be seen contentedly munching the lush grass studded with wild flowers which grow here, a perfect picture for tourist cameras. You pass The Secret Garden (highly recommended) to reach the starting point of the walk.

Gorey Castle

Or Mont Orgueil, as it is more properly known, is undoubtedly Jersey's most impressive spectacle. Continually fortified from the time Normandy was lost to King John in 1204 until the German Occupation of 1940-45, the castle is an object lesson in the evolution of defence against seige and a microcosm of the history of the nation. This book is not the place for a lengthy exposition of the story of Gorey Castle – far better for anyone interested to visit the castle, where an imaginative and inspiring display, with tableaux and audio-visual effects, brings the castle to life in a way which mere words cannot.

Gorey

May not be Jersey's second town (that distinction must belong to Red Houses/Quennevais in the parish of St Brelade) but it is most definitely a community with an identity and atmosphere all its own. It is clearly a focal point for the eastern side of the island, the side which faces France; various craft work the passage between Gorey and a number of ports in Normandy and, in the season, the streets of Gorey often sound more French than English.

Gorey has two foci: one is the harbour with its terrace of houses/shops/restaurants picturesquely arranged above the harbour wall and beneath Mont Orgueil. The second is the village centre with quite a range of shops which cater to the needs of the locals rather than tourists. Here, too, is to be found the Jersey Pottery, deservedly one of the island's premier attractions.

QUEEN'S VALLEY RESERVOIR

This walk, by a landscaped footpath which circumnavigates the recently created reservoir in Queen's Valley, is an enjoyable and undemanding walk. The traverse across the dam at the valley mouth makes for a fairly memorable half way mark.

Start: Car park at head of Queen's Valley Reservoir
Map reference: 699507
Bus: No 3A, 20 to St. Saviour's Hospital
Parking: Car park at head of reservoir
Distance: 2 kilometres

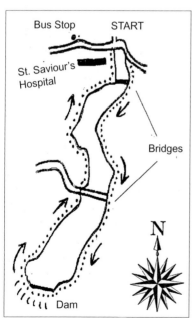

From the car park at the head of Queen's Valley Reservoir you must first decide which way you wish to walk round the reservoir – clockwise or anti-clockwise. If clockwise then head towards the gate to the left and follow the grit track as it climbs through the trees above the water. This is a pleasantly undulating path, never tedious – and with the added interest of varied woodland close at hand. As you traverse the dam you can see clearly that it is built across the mouth of the former Queen's Valley. The grassy slope reaches down to a neatly landscaped pond and former mill. Beyond is a view across the flat lands of Grouville-Les Marais – with the spire of Grouville Church and the tower of the former windmill, Le Moulin de Beauvoir – on the skyline beyond.

The track back to the head of the reservoir is rather different in character: at first it is directly above the water, having been hacked out of the steep valley side. Later it negotiates a number of inlets and is flanked with vegetation.

Eventually the rear elevation of St. Saviour's Hospital looms into view as you reach the car park at the head of the reservoir, with its resident population of water fowl.

Queen's Valley was a lovely unspoilt valley before they built the reservoir. George Eliot enthused over it when she visited Jersey in 1857, describing Queen's Valley as 'a broad strip of meadow and pasture lies between two high slopes covered with woods and ferney wilderness. Everywhere there are tethered cows looking at you with meek faces.' Anyone who can remember the valley before the Great Flood will do so with a fondness for a slice of rural Jersey that has been lost forever.

Gorey Castle, or Mont Orgueil

Walk 4

GOREY HARBOUR CIRCULAR

*Gorey Harbour via Jeffrey's Leap, Victoria Tower,
Dolmen de Faldouet and Le Mont St. Nicolas*

This is a short walk packed with interest and unforgettable views. There is a steep ascent from the road at Jeffrey's Leap to the Victoria Tower but otherwise the going is easy.

Start:	Gorey Harbour
Map Reference:	714503
Bus:	No 1 to terminus at Gorey Harbour
Parking:	Gorey Harbour or the approach road to the harbour
Distance:	2 kilometres

With your back to the terrace of buildings facing Gorey Harbour turn right, away from the harbour. Immediately past the public conveniences turn right and climb the path (signposted '**To Gorey Castle**') behind the buildings to reach the attractive Castle Green. Carry straight on until you reach the road heading north. Unfortunately the pavement soon runs out but you have not far to go on the road, which bends to the left and soon reaches the rocky outcrop known as **Jeffrey's Leap**, with its fine view over Anne Port and the rest of St. Catherine's Bay, partly enclosed by the magnificent breakwater.

Just before the now deserted **Jeffrey's Leap Tea Rooms**, on the opposite side of the road, look out for a Jersey National Trust sign indicating '**Le Don Pilkington**'. Cross the road and climb the steps up the steep bank. Your efforts are well rewarded as you emerge by **Victoria Tower** with its tremendously wide views.

Walk beyond the Tower and bear right along a track past the house to reach a minor junction with Seymour Farm on the right.

Bear right at **Seymour Farm** and walk a little way along the lane, looking out to the left for a sign erected by La Société Jersiaise indicating the entrance path leading to the **Dolmen de Faldouet**, with its enormous capstone, set in a peaceful, hedge-rimmed enclosure and looking out across fields to the open sea.

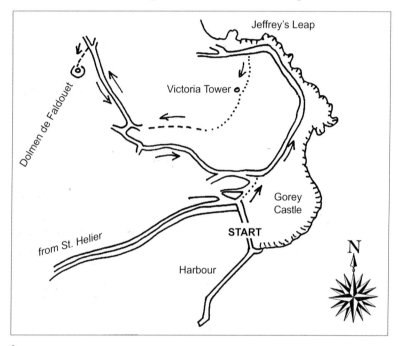

After contemplating the dolmen and its views you retrace your steps to the junction at Seymour Farm where you bear right, then sharp left to descend the lane towards Gorey Harbour. In my view, the head of this lane is the best possible vantage point from which to appreciate the commanding presence and noble outline of Gorey Castle, or Mont Orgueil (Mount Pride), as it is otherwise known. This lane is used only for access so your peace should be preserved – a bench seat is even provided for your ease. As you descend further towards Castle Green you will notice the eponymous pub with its fine views.

Jeffrey's Leap: The promontory which forms the southern flank of Anne Port, is so called because an unfortunate Jeffrey was condemned to be thrown off the cliff here as punishment for a crime. However, he took the law into his own hands, jumped into the sea and swam ashore, only to be recaptured. He jumped off the cliff once more but this time the tide had turned, in every sense, and he was dashed to pieces on the uncovered rocks below.

Jersey National Trust: Yes, Jersey has its own National Trust, founded in 1936, which owns and protects a surprisingly large number of buildings and tracts of land. Wherever you see its attractive logo (see page 12), featuring a Martello tower, you will usually find it accompanied by a sign indicating, 'Le Don ... ', as in Le Don Pilkington opposite Jeffrey's Leap. 'Le Don Pilkington' simply means 'the gift of', in this case, 'Dr. Roger Pilkington', this hillside having been donated to the Trust by the good Dr. P.

Victoria Tower was the last of the Jersey towers, having been erected in 1837, soon after which peace at last broke out between Britain and France. It is curious in that it is surrounded by a dry moat, the entrance door being reached by a drawbridge. The tower is now topped by a telescope used by Victoria College Astronomical Group.

*Dolmen
at
Faldouet*

Dolmen de Faldouet: Like that at Mont Ubé, is the property of La Société Jersiaise. Three centuries ago, an observer recorded that it was still covered by a mound of earth; when it was later excavated the passage was found to lead to a number of human bones. Most of the upright stones are composed of local granite but the massive capstone, estimated to weigh 23 tons, is rhyolite, a volcanic rock which outcrops about a quarter of a mile to the north.

Martello Tower at Archirondel

EAST COAST PATH

*Gorey to St. Catherine's Breakwater via Anne Port,
Archirondel and La Mare.*

The coastscape here is not as spectacular as it is on the other sides of the island but it has its own appeal and interest and I have attempted to denote its character in my Introduction by the phrase, 'pastoral and intimate'. If you walk this stretch of the coast I hope you will see what I mean. There are beach cafés at Archirondel and St Catherine's.

Start:	Gorey Harbour
Map Reference:	714503
Bus:	No 1 to terminus at Gorey Harbour; No 1B from St. Catherine's Breakwater
Parking:	Gorey Harbour or the approach road to the harbour
Distance:	4 kilometres

From Gorey Harbour you begin the walk by taking the path which rises immediately after the public conveniences to cross Castle Green, and reaches the road north to **Jeffrey's Leap** (see Walk 4). Again, at **Anne Port**, the road must be followed as it skirts between the sea wall and the bosky slopes on the landward side.

Follow the road around the next headland, past the barbecue emplacements, and follow the grassy bank past the former **Les Arches Hotel,** currently awaiting redevelopment, nicely framed by the wooded côtil behind. The grassy bank soon peters out but, not very much farther on, you will spot a sign indicating '**Archirondel Beach and Cafe, 100 yards**' to the right and it will be a small relief to realise that the route from here all the way to St. Catherine's Breakwater is entirely by footpath.

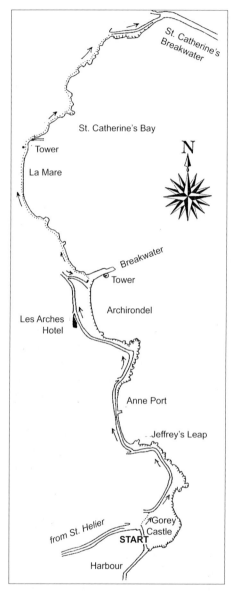

At the end of the patio in front of the **Driftwood Café** you climb to the top of the sea wall and follow this all the way to the Martello tower at La Mare. At certain points this sea wall is quite a height above the beach and, as it has no protective railing, CARE SHOULD BE TAKEN, particularly if you have children with you.

Just on the far side of the very long slipway at La Mare you will observe the indicated footpath just to the right of the road. It begins on top of the sea wall, such as it is, and is delightfully varied in its course, crossing Conglomerate where delicate, pink sea thrift seems to grow out of the bare rock to contrast picturesquely with yellow lichen. You will skirt some unbelievably small potato fields, one of which must surely rank as the tiniest cultivated field in the island.

At **St. Catherine's Breakwater** there is a café and a commemorative stone dating the breakwater and its splendid masonry – 1847. This point is where the paths to Fliquet begin, described in the next Walk - No 6.

Anne Port: This small bay, without so much as a beach café or a deck chair, is a personal favourite. At mid- and low-tide a fine sandy beach is exposed and the gentle shelving here makes for good swimming. You will notice the very distinctive deep red colours of the cobbles piled up against the sea wall – indeed, the sea wall is composed of large pieces of the same rock, volcanic rhyolite, though the coping stones are the more familiar granite.

St. Catherine
from
Le Malade

Slipways: Or simply 'slips', are an ubiquitous feature of the Jersey coastline. They act as a link between coast road and beach. Some are very long (is the one at La Mare/ St. Catherine's the longest?); some are straight, others curved; some run parallel to the sea wall whilst others aim directly for the sea; one or two are even forked, and all are a lasting monument to the mason's craft. Slipways were used mainly by farmers to bring their carts to the beach in order to collect *vraic* (ie. seaweed, pronounced 'rack') for use as fertiliser, and the paving stones are set at an angle which allowed horses' hooves to gain purchase.

Rozel Conglomerate is a coarse formation – a conglomeration of rock fragments bound up in a matrix of once molten rock – which forms the north-eastern corner of Jersey. This distinctive geological formation has a reddish hue and all the appearance of a giant's pudding mixture. Its genesis is obscure but it is certainly the youngest of Jersey's various rocks – we know this because it contains fragments of all the other local rocks. A good place to observe the Rozel Conglomerate is in the rocks behind St. Catherine's Breakwater.

Carved stones built into a buttress, St. Martin's Church.
How many faces can you find?

ROSEL WOODS CIRCULAR

La Mare via St. Catherine's Reservoir and St. Martin's Village.
Alternative route: Linear walk from La Mare to St. Martin's Church.

This is a lovely inland walk through a thickly wooded valley which eventually rises to St. Martin's Village where you can find a pub and shop. The return can be varied by taking a different route for about half the journey. St. Catherine's Reservoir is no vast undertaking, being not much more than a pond. There is a great variety of wild flowers on this walk.

Start:	La Mare, St. Catherine's Bay
Map Reference:	704524
Bus:	No.1B to La Mare
	Alternative return: No. 3, 3A from
	St. Martin's Church
Parking:	There is a public car park beside the road
	by the Martello tower
Distance:	5 kilometres

From the road at **La Mare**, with your back to the sea, turn left, then right at the junction, then immediately fork left along the track. Once past the houses, the track becomes a pot-holed dirt track and then narrows to a footpath. Pass the diminutive reservoir, tread stepping stones to cross a stream and then simply follow the path up along the valley. You may notice the outcrops of Rozel Conglomerate beside the path.

Further along the footpath changes in character: instead of being entirely shrouded by trees you look out on to a more open, boggy valley bottom on your right with a stream running through it, with lots of irises lending a splash of yellow when in flower.

33

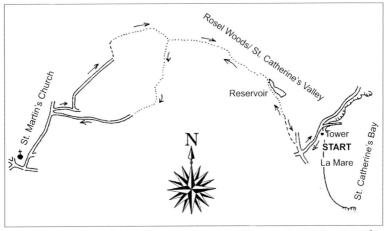

As you reach a little pond and a Private Property sign the path forks. Take the left fork and follow the path until it joins a lane – carry on in the same direction, ascending gently, past a *lavoir*, a place for washing household linen, and *abreuvoir*, an animal drinking place. The spire of St. Martin's Church comes into view beyond the pasture on your left. At the T-junction you may turn left to reach St. Martin's Church, the pub, the village stores and the No. 3 bus stop.

But, to continue the circular walk, as you emerge from the lane – **Rue des Vaux de l'Eglise** – turn right, past **Ash Cottage**, then sharp right along **Rue Belin** and past the rather stark façade of the **Wesleyan Chapel**, dated 1850. If you look inside you will notice that the Bible inscriptions on the wall behind the altar are in French.

Just past the chapel follow the lane by bearing left, then right, then bear left at the T-junction ahead. Follow the lane as it bears right above the wooded valley and becomes a footpath. (According to the O.S. map, these valley paths are designated as bridleways).

The path gradually descends, crosses the very narrow lane in the valley bottom and continues until it rejoins the point where you forked left on your outward journey; from here on simply retrace your steps along the valley bottom, past the reservoir and back to the road and **La Mare**.

Lavoir and abreuvoir, Vallée Jenne. The granite pillar is inscribed with the date 1846 and sets of initials detailing its founders.

Rosel Woods: Also known as St. Catherine's Valley, is a wooded valley running roughly east/west, connecting St. Catherine's Bay at La Mare with St. Martin's village. At the start of the walk up the valley you pass a dammed pond; this is in fact a small reservoir constructed by the Germans during the Occupation.

St. Martin's Village is set about a crossing of main roads. The church, with its plain stone spire, stands at its heart, and close by is the customary group of Parish School, Parish Room, shop and pub. The Church has a grandeur which points to the fact that it was once considered the leading church in the island. Curiously, its spire has twice been destroyed by lightning, in 1616 and 1837, and twice rebuilt, the second time with a lightning conductor.

I am grateful to G.R. Balleine (*The Bailiwick of Jersey:* Hodder, 1951) for the following story which, as he points out, provides an amusing instance of Jersey thrift: 'In 1749 we find The Churchwardens petitioned the Ecclesiastical Court for permission to substitute windows for two of their doors. They explained that they had four doors but only two Almoners; and at whichever door they stationed these officers to take the collection, many of the congregation slipped out through the others.'

Methodism in Jersey: The Methodist movement of the late eighteenth century set firm roots in the Channel Islands, with their Presbyterian tradition of non-conformity. At first, Methodism was confined to English residents, but John Wesley had a profound influence on the inhabitants of Jersey and Guernsey when he visited the islands in 1787. Once some of the bilingual islanders were converted the movement spread rapidly. There was opposition from the authorities however, particularly on the issue of military drills on the Sabbath, but the Methodist cause was eventually won. Many chapels, some of massive proportions and built in the classical style, are still to be seen in Jersey and many have active congregations. The non-conformist influence on island life is perhaps more evident in Guernsey where the pubs still shut on Sundays, much to the consternation of the uninitiated holidaymaker.

Wesleyan Chapel, St. Martin's

ST. CATHERINE'S CIRCULAR

St. Catherine's Breakwater via Fliquet

This very short walk is really no more than a stroll from the head of St. Catherine's Breakwater to Fliquet just to the north. A pair of footpaths link the unfrequented Fliquet with the much-visited St. Catherine's, and I would be missing an opportunity if I were not to point out these ways in the present book. This short walk can constitute a pleasant diversion from the *cul de sac* of St. Catherine's. There are no buses from Fliquet nor, as yet, is there a coast path beyond Fliquet so, for completeness, it is recommended that you should reach Fliquet on one path and return to St. Catherine's on the other.

Bus:	Parking:
Map Reference:	715531
Bus:	No. 1B to terminus to St. Catherine's
Parking:	There are a number of parking places in the vicinity of the Café
Distance:	1 kilometre

Just beyond the start of the breakwater you will find the entrance to the **two paths to Fliquet**, an upper and a lower path. The lower path is occasionally closed off, being vulnerable to the demands of a sometimes angry sea. If it is open, and you are feeling adventurous, it is a delightful route, with trees and genuine wild daffodils reaching down the hillsides to the high tide mark.

The upper path takes you through a charming park-like landscape to join a lane which drops down to the (concrete!)

slipway at Fliquet. It is worth examining the beach here as you may find exposed a layer of peat in which you can find such objects as beetle cases. Alas, Fliquet marks the end of the coast path in this direction. There is a missing link between here and La Coupe which, it is hoped, will one day be completed.

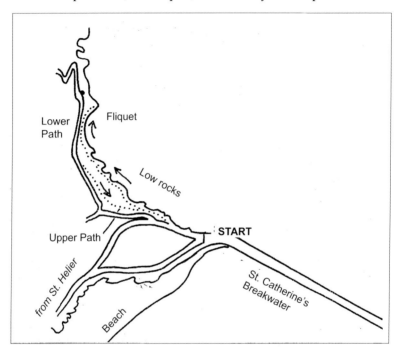

Fliquet is, in effect, the beginning of Jersey's rocky northern coastline but it was felt that a Martello tower was needed to defend the comparatively low-lying hinterland. At certain states of the tide you may be able to find a bed of peat outcropping among the shingle and between the rocks of Rozel Conglomerate. This formation is known as head, and contains a fossil fauna and flora which indicates its genesis at the close of the last Ice Age, more than 25,000 years ago. There is no path from Fliquet to La Coupe, though it is possible to negotiate the low rocks when the tide is out. La Coupe is very much one of the more remote and less frequented corners of the island.

St. Catherine's Breakwater: The island's longest breakwater is also Jersey's great folly. It was constructed between 1847 and 1855 to be used as a Naval base (officially 'a harbour of refuge'). The area enclosed promptly silted up and the harbour was never used, though it is today much appreciated by local anglers and provides a pleasant, easy stroll.

Breakwater with massive masonry at St. Catherine's

The Ecréhous (pronounced in Jersey: 'eck-ree-ose') are a group of small islands which lie midway between Normandy and Jersey's north-east coast. The whole reef comprises some nine square miles when uncovered at low water. On a clear day, with the sun shining down, the huddle of buildings on Marmoutier, one of the larger islands, looks alarmingly like the back street of an old town afloat in the open sea.

The highest point on Maitre Ile, the largest island, is sixty feet above sea level. There was an ecclesiatical settlement here in medieval times, though little now remains. Apart from the occasional hermit, the islets are inhabited only by itinerant fishermen. The once vexed question of their ownership was finally settled by the Hague Tribunal in 1953 which decided in favour of Britain, though it seems that certain French fishermen have never quite accepted this verdict.

Walk 8
L'ETACQ CIRCULAR

*via Dolmen des Monts Grantez, Les Vaux Cuissin
and La Rue de la Mare*

This is an undemanding walk which explores a little known corner
of the island which, in the season, is a good place for blackberrying.

Start: Car park opposite 'Treasures of the Earth"
Map Reference: 563541
Bus: No. 12A to 'Treasures of the Earth'
Parking: Car park opposite 'Treasures of the Earth'
Distance: 5 kilometres

The Walk begins at the public car park opposite 'Treasures of
the Earth' at the foot of Mont Pinel. A useful starting point is the
Information Board in the corner of the car park which displays a
map and description of **Les Mielles Conservation Zone**. Just
behind this display is a beaten path leading past a small pond to
an opening on to the road to the right. Cross here (mind the traffic)
and make for the signposted footpath on the far side.

The right of way comprises a narrow path which skirts the
right hand side of the quarry face and works. Beyond the quarry
the path ascends some steps under a crag, from which a great
wide view opens up across St. Ouen's, Jersey's widest bay.

To continue the walk: follow the beaten path across this
uncultivated, open land – **La Grande Thiebault; Jersey National
Trust** – towards the white house ahead. Follow the track, past
the bungalow on the left and look out for a signpost on the right
indicating access to the **Dolmen des Monts Grantez**, which may
be found within a walled enclosure nearby. You will see the spire
of St. Ouen's Church from here and, beyond it, that of St. Peter's.

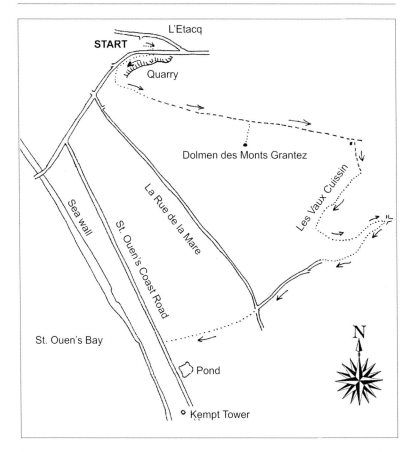

Continue along the track, now metalled, until you reach a bungalow on your right called **Les Vaux Cuissin**. Just past here turn right to follow the signposted footpath beside the privet hedge; where the hedge ends you bear right and follow the sandy path above Les Vaux Cuissin, now the real thing, with views seawards beyond Kempt Tower to the open sea. Follow steps down to the valley bottom, cross a footbridge and continue by the path on the far side as it curves around a promontory.

You soon reach a junction of ways – bear right here, not along the level track, but by the lower, narrower path on the more extreme right, which descends between walls of brambles and bracken.

Join the lane and carry on until you reach a minor road – La **Rue de la Mare** – where you turn right. Follow this quiet back road until you reach a junction on the main road where it is but a short distance to the car park where we began the walk.

Alternatively, upon reaching La Rue de la Mare, you may carry on towards St. Ouen's Bay by crossing the common land between here and the bay. To do this, bear right along La Rue de la Mare; as you approach the houses on the right go through the gate on the left or, failing that, cross the double step stile opposite the house called **St. Antony**.

Les Mielles: Refers to the large tract of land behind St. Ouen's Bay consisting mainly of sand dunes and the slopes of the plateau to the east, and is afforded special protection against development in order to conserve its landscape and unique fauna and flora, as well as its numerous prehistoric remains. Before this, especially prior to the Occupation, many buildings of doubtful merit sprang up in this spacious and sparsely populated quarter of the island (though the Germans flattened any that were in their line of fire), and there has been a great deal of sand excavation.

The flora, in particular, is rich and extremely varied, the island, with its favourable climate, having afforded sustenance to plants native to the British Isles, the European continent, the Mediterranean, the Iberian Peninsula, even from southern Africa, making Les Mielles a botanist's paradise. St. Ouen's Pond, or La Mare au Seigneur, is the largest natural body of fresh water on the island and is an important bird reserve. Pretty much the whole of Les Mielles is open to the public, though some ecologically sensitive areas are fenced off.

Dolmen des Monts Grantez enjoys, typically for Jersey dolmens, a fine, wide view. This dolmen was capped by a mound as late as 1912, when it was excavated to reveal a roofed passage leading to an oval chamber with smaller side cell. The remains of eight or nine bodies were also found, together with offerings of limpet shells and pebbles from the beach selected for their beauty.

KEMPT TOWER CIRCULAR

via St. Ouen's Church and Mont Matthieu

This is a delightful route, heading directly inland from St Ouen's Bay, first across the sand dunes of Les Mielles, then by what has all the feel of an ancient track up a minor valley to reach La Ville au Bas. Soon after this we take an unmade track which leads directly to St. Ouen's Church, and return to the bay by a usually quiet lane and the hairpin bends of Mont Matthieu with its spectacular views.

Start:	Kempt Tower
Map Reference:	563525
Bus:	No. 12A to Kempt Tower
Parking:	Car park beside Kempt Tower
Distance:	5 kilometres

From **Kempt Tower**, with your back to the sea, bear left and cross the road. Once past the small reeded pond and just before the bungalow head inland and continue along the sandy track beside the boundary fence of the pond, soon signposted as **Bird Reserve**.

Carry on along the main beaten path directly inland, passing the parking place with barbecue emplacements to the left. You cross another track running from left to right and make for the footpath and bridleway signs ahead, the two parallel ways separated by a growth of tree lupins. When you reach **La Rue de la Mare**, the metalled lane, cross over and follow the sandy track straight ahead towards the plateau, passing sand pits on the right. The track rises gradually and reaches a fork: bear left along the bramble-banked track towards the modern house.

Follow the track as it bears right between low, lichen-encrusted

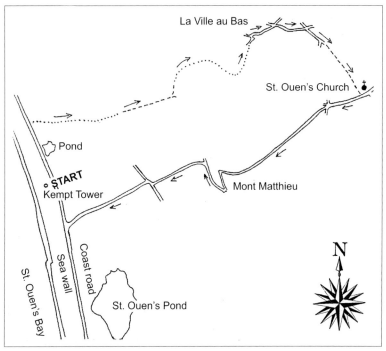

dry stone walls which support a lush growth of pennywort. The next section of this track can be rather muddy – a stream flows beside the track, first on the left, then on the right. The track becomes a narrow path, passes a small reservoir on the right and soon emerges onto a lane and a group of buildings known as **La Ville au Bas**. Follow the lane beside the slated roofs and turn right at the crossing of ways, along an unmade track which emerges at a lane – turn right here along **Rue du Couvent**. Notice the tower to the right – this marks the site of a former windmill.

Soon the lane bears right, but you go straight ahead by the rough track between stone walls, walls which, with their topping of turf out of which sprouts a jungle of ivy, gorse, brambles and pennywort, remind one of Cornwall or Brittany. This track leads directly to the three gables and squat spire of **St. Ouen's Church**.

Leave the churchyard and bear right along the lane which gradually descends **Mont Matthieu** towards St. Ouen's Bay, the view widening as you proceed. At the first hairpin bend you will no doubt wish to pause beside the lane to take in the view over Les Mielles and ahead to Kempt Tower. Follow the lane to the left and right around the sharp bends, then left again to reach **La Rue de la Mare** where you go straight on along **Chemin de L'Ouzière** to reach the main road and Kempt Tower. Look out for the White Menhir a short distance to the right. There is a bus stop along the coast road to the left.

Kempt Tower or La Grosse Tour is a former Martello tower which now houses an extensive display featuring Les Mielles Conservation Zone, and is well worth a visit. There are a number of exhibits depicting all aspects of the landscape, ecology, history and prehistory of the area and a number of explanatory leaflets are available. You may also join a number of walks which are run from here. The tower itself is worthy of inspection – it is massively built of granite; access to the roof provides a fine viewpoint.

St. Ouen's Church and Parish is named after St. Ouen, an Archbishop of Rouen in the seventh century; a tiny splinter of his bone comprised the relic deemed necessary in those days in order that an altar might be consecrated and a church founded. The church therefore dates from pre-Norman times and was regarded as the property of the de Carterets, the local Seigneurs or 'lords of the Manor', St. Ouen's Manor being their seat. This beautifully kept and well used church has a long and eventful history and time should be taken to explore within.

St. Ouen is Jersey's largest parish. It is also the most remote from St. Helier and many local people are of the opinion that the St. Ouennais are a race apart, the true Jerseymen (or not), speaking with a broader accent and even possessing a distinct version of Jersey Norman-French.

If there is a village of St. Ouen's, its shops and pub are grouped around the Parish Hall on the main road to the north of the church. The buildings near the church are now all residential (apart from the art shop) which is a pity, but the hamlet retains the special feel of St. Ouen's parish – of remoteness and exposure to the elements – which is lacking in the 'high town'.

LE VAL DE LA MARE RESERVOIR

This is an unusual walk around Jersey's 'Lake District' – a well landscaped reservoir encircled by a public footpath with opportunity to digress into quiet cul de sacs.

Start: Car park at head of Le Val beside main road
Map Reference: 589527
Bus: No. 9 to Le Val de la Mare
Parking: Car park at head of Le Val beside main road.
Distance: 5 kilometres

The start of this walk is reached from the car park off the main road – La Grand Route de St. Pierre, designated Jersey's A12, which links Beaumont with the village centres of St. Peter and St. Ouen. This is almost directly opposite the beautifully restored house known as La Hougue. A noticeboard in the car park indicates this as the Pedestrians Only entrance to **Val de la Mare Reservoir** and its **Arboretum**.

Follow the gravel footpath as it leads gently down beside the stream towards the reservoir, or you may digress to left and right by way of secondary paths which have been hacked out of the bosky slopes and run parallel to the main path. The boggy ground beside the stream is a good place to identify a wealth of moisture loving plants. Just before you reach the reservoir itself, you will encounter the beginning of an alternative path which follows the north bank. If you are in no particular hurry I would recommend this as the more interesting and varied way.

Climb up this path and follow the way as it skirts arable fields to the right and strides above slopes crowded with bracken and brambles and young fir trees. Soon the view opens out and you can see across the water to the dam and further across Les Mielles towards the open sea.

The path follows a promontory and a major arm of the reservoir which points north towards the spire of St Ouen's Church. At the head of this inlet is a seat from which the view back over the water is really quite impressive – you could almost imagine yourself in the English Lake District! Reservoirs can be most attractive when they are full and the water is brimming to meet the green slopes on either side but are not nearly as impressive when an unsightly tide mark separates the water from the greenery (as in the drawing overleaf).

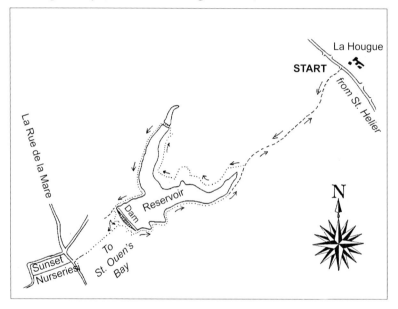

Simply follow the path until you reach the dam. You used to be able to cross the top of the dam – a short walk which injected a shot of real drama into this circular ramble. Now, unfortunately, locked gates prevent your experiencing this and, if you wish to complete the circular route you must descend the hairpin path below the dam, access to which is gained just past the dam on your left, then cross the field below and climb up the far side, a somewhat laborious business.

Alternatively, you can descend the path below the dam and continue seawards to reach the lane. **La Rue de la Mare** is to the right, that interesting lane which follows a course parallel to the sea front road but set well back between the flat fields and the plateau. You will find **Sunset Nurseries** across the road at the T-junction. This is a pleasantly laid-back tourist attraction which is well worth a visit. It is an ideal place to see Jersey's carnation growing industry in action.

You can follow a quiet lane, La Route de la Marette, from here between the fields. Just before you pass the flooded sand pit you can see the standing stone known as the **White Menhir** a short distance to the right. There is a bus stop along the coast road to the left.

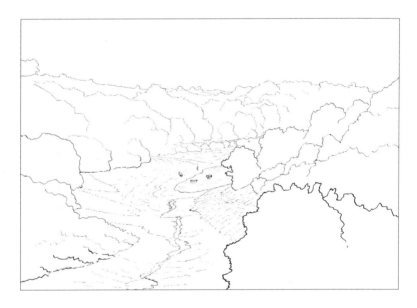

Low water in the reservoir, Val de la Mare

LE BRAYE CIRCULAR

*via La Pulente, Le Petit Port, the Railway Walk
and Les Quenneuais*

This is an interesting and extremely varied route which takes in the quiet southern end of St. Ouen's Bay, a good section of the delightful Railway Walk and the strange and distinct dune landscape of Les Quennevais.

Start:	Le Braye
Map Reference:	566501
Bus:	No. 12A to Le Braye
Parking:	Car park at Le Braye
Distance:	7 kilometres

From **Le Braye slipway** head south towards **Corbière Lighthouse**. There is a soft shoulder of partly grassed sand dunes between the road and the sea wall which runs for almost a mile to the slipway at La Pulente; this is a good place to spot the famous Jersey green lizard and provides a pleasant walk along an undulating coastal strip looking down onto a sandy beach and, further out at low tide, a wide expanse of low rocks.

About half way along here you will encounter a Second World War gun emplacement and a quarry face on the far side of the road. Join the road just above the slipway at **La Pulente** and walk for a short distance beside the road until it takes a hairpin bend to the left and you reach the beginning of the coast path around the promontory jutting out to sea. Immediately you have a choice of ways – you can either follow the coast path, on an even contour, around the promontory, or you can climb the steps by a permissive footpath which crosses over the top.

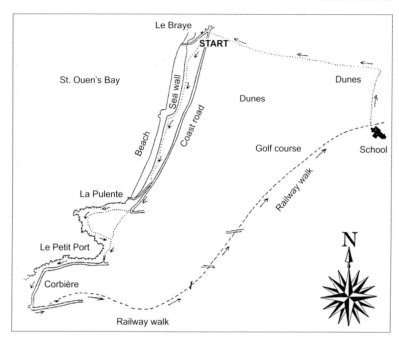

- Whichever way you choose, you will reach the same point on
- the far side, with its view over **Le Petit Port**, a rock-strewn cove
- complete with slipway. Now follow the beaten path as it bears
- right through the vegetation behind the slipway until you reach
- the main road which you must now follow towards Corbière.

Gun emplacement, Le Petit Port, north of Corbière

It is possible, at low tide, to take the path which leads off the road to reach the lighthouse. But beware, the causeway between rocks to the lighthouse is covered either side of high tide. A bell sounds to warn of the rising tide. If you hear this bell do not risk crossing to the lighthouse – the tide rises rapidly around Jersey and the cross-currents here are treacherous.

From Corbière follow the road uphill in an easterly direction. To your right you can see a German-built tower and, further east, Jersey's Desalination Plant where, in times of drought, sea water is distilled to produce fresh water. You will notice a toilet block on your right; on your left is a pull-in for buses at the Corbière terminus. Bear left here to reach the beginning (or end!) of the **Railway Walk**. You may notice a few sections of rail around here poking out of the ground among the bushes. But the best clue to the origin of the path is the former station building on the right beside the old track – the long low platform is obvious.

Now follow the Railway Walk for about two miles. The path gradually rises between the fir trees (many of which have been replanted following the 1987 Hurricane). Pass the **golf course** (La Moye Golf Club) which is laid out on the sand dunes, and continue between a wooded area (left) and some houses (right). The point at which the route leaves the Railway Walk is identified by the large modern school buildings on the right and the playing fields on the left. Look out for a path along a miniature avenue of pines which heads off to the left, between the boundary of the playing fields (to the right) and that of the golf course (left).

Continue along here until the avenue ends and the boundary fence of the golf course takes a sharp left hand turn. Cross the stile and, as if by magic, enter a completely different landscape. This is Les Quennevais, the most impressive portion of Les Mielles Conservation Zone, where the sand dunes reach Saharan proportions and support a unique flora, much of it only evident to the observer prepared to get down on hands and knees. The presence of shells and shell fragments in the sand points to the origin of these dunes as the child of sea and wind and which, in this vicinity, are called appropriately Les Blanches Banques.

The dunes are criss-crossed with paths (or are many of them rabbit runs?) and you should perhaps sit awhile in this strange landscape, if only to indulge your Beau Geste fantasies. Children (and occasionally adults) love rolling down the steep soft sand slopes.

Les Blanches Banques

So, there is no set path across these dunes and you are free to wander at will – but do respect the areas newly planted with marram grass in an attempt to stabilise the dunes and prevent the many blow-outs which are evident. When you are in a position to see ahead, if you head towards La Rocco Tower in St Ouen's Bay you will be heading back towards Le Braye, but there is plenty of interest on the way. Not least of these are the various standing stones which are dispersed among the dunes. Keep heading west and you will reach the road and the bus stop and facilities at Le Braye.

Corbière: All vessels approaching Jersey from the mainland and the other islands must negotiate the rocky south-western corner of the island which faces the prevailing winds. Many a ship was wrecked here before the States of Jersey built a lighthouse in 1873. An outlying rock was chosen to build a concrete platform as the base for a 35 feet high tower – the first lighthouse in the British Isles to be built of concrete. The light can be seen for many miles and must have saved countless ships from disaster. Corbière Lighthouse, set squarely on the pink granite rock, is an inspiring vision which has become a symbol of Jersey.

Corbière Lighthouse

La Rocco Tower: One of the Martello towers built to counter potential invasion from Revolutionary and then Napoleonic France, in this case on an off-shore rock. It was used for artillery practice by the Germans during the Occupation and subsequently rebuilt. It now forms the emblem of the Les Mielles Conservation Zone.

MONT A LA BRUNE - LE BRAYE

● ●

via Le Mont Crapaud

This route follows a signposted bridleway which leaves Le Mont à la Brune and follows an undulating course with some good views of the singular landscape of Les Blanches Banques to reach St. Ouen's Bay and the coast road at Le Braye.

Start:	Turning into Mont à la Brune from Airport road
Map Reference:	586503
Bus:	No. 15 to Mont à la Brune, No 12A from Le Braye
Parking:	No car park or road parking – this is a walk for pedestrians only
Distance:	3 kilometres

From the main road head down **Le Mont à la Brune** which, in its upper reaches, forms the boundary of the Airport as it begins to descend a pleasant unspoilt valley towards St. Ouen's Bay.

Keep a sharp look out for the entrance to a signposted Bridlepath on the left, complete with a granite block inscribed **Les Mielles**. Follow the way as it climbs and circles the little promontory indicated on the O.S. map as Le Mont Crapaud, blanketed with brambles but not enough to obscure the views. This is an excellent vantage point for Les Blanches Banques, the giant sand hills spread out to the south.

It is possible to wander at will hereabouts but, to continue the walk, you descend the hillside, then bear seawards once more, first beside an enclave of modern houses on your right, then

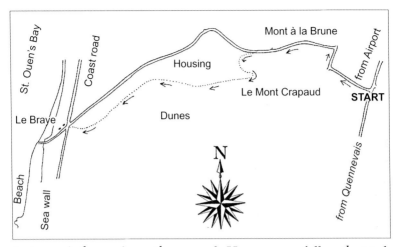

- towards the road near the car park. Here you can follow the track
- among the low dunes to avoid the road altogether until you reach
- the coast road at Le Braye.

Le Mont Crapaud is an interesting appellation since 'crapaud' is the name of the large Jersey toad, once so common on the island that 'Crapaud' became the nickname for a Jerseyman. The view towards Les Blanches Banques from here is certainly very striking. These sandhills are the closest Jersey approaches to a mountain landscape. On a misty day the receding outlines of each successive group of hills are reduced to a number of dark lines so that the impression of size and height is greatly enhanced.

Standing Stone, below
Les Blanches Banques

St. Brelade's Church

ST. BRELADE'S - BEAUPORT

This short walk explores a special portion of Jersey's south-west corner, from its most picturesquely situated parish church of St. Brelade's, peeping through trees across its beautiful sandy bay, to the perfect cove of Beauport.

Start:	St. Brelade's Parish Church
Map Reference:	582484
Bus:	Nos. 12, 14 to St. Brelade's Bay
Parking:	Car park just uphill from St. Brelade's Church
Distance:	2 kilometres

You may wish to begin this walk by exploring the **Parish Church** of St. Brelade and the ancient **Fishermen's Chapel** which adjoins it. On leaving the churchyard bear left up the lane towards La Saline, not by the road straight ahead to Beauport. Look out for a Footpath sign on the right. This introduces a pedestrian way over the headland above La Saline, with wide views across St. Brelade's and the wooded slopes behind the bay.

This path eventually reaches a lane where you bear left to reach the car park above **Beauport**. You can scramble down the stepped path to the bay or continue along the cliff-top path to the next promontory, and it is well worth doing so. The granite rock formations here are awesome, with great stacks of jointed rock perched precariously above the waves. Les Caines reef is scattered not far out to sea to the south-west.

There is no circular walk available here and you must retrace your steps – though it is surprising how differently the scene can appear approached from the opposite direction and this superlative stroll will surely please you both going and coming back.

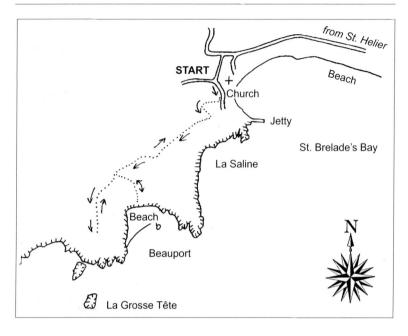

Rock formations from the headland beyond Beauport

⬤
⬤   Alternatively, you could follow the minor lane from the car
⬤   park at Beauport to reach a T-junction where your turn right to
⬤   descend to St. Brelade's Church.

Beauport is my all time favourite. Totally unspoiled – and long may it remain so – it is reached only by a steep climb down from the cliff top which steers you along a sandy path through bracken. Perfectly smooth granite cobbles of pink and beige, like giant sugar almonds, form a storm beach, followed by firm sand, washed clean twice daily by the tide. The gradient of the beach means the sea is never far away and the swimming is ideal at all states of the tide. There are endless nooks and crannies to be explored around the bay's containing walls, as well as the monumental rock formation at the bay's nodal point to be contemplated at any time, surrounded either by water or by sand, according to the tide. Beauport is the perfect place for keeping yourself fully occupied whilst doing absolutely nothing!

St. Brelade's Church is the only one of Jersey's twelve parish churches which is built right on the coast and enjoys an unfettered view across the sea. It is tucked into a sheltered corner of St. Brelade's Bay, close by the harbour, and for this reason is perhaps the most memorable of all. Originally, two small chapels were built side by side in the churchyard. One, a private chantry, remains much as it was and is known as the Fishermen's Chapel, the medieval paintings which decorated its walls now restored. The other grew and developed over the centuries into the present parish church. St. Brelade is a corruption of St. Brendan, the great Celtic missionary. The parish of St. Brelade comprises the entire south-west chunk of Jersey, from St. Aubin to St. Ouen, and includes Noirmont, Portelet, Beauport, Corbière and Les Blanches Banques. As such, the parish is surely one of Jersey's most varied and attractive.

BEAUPORT - CORBIÈRE

This stretch of coastal footpath, much of which has only recently been made officially accessible, covers the Island's wild south-west corner. It's regrettable the route is home to such unpicturesque but necessary buildings as the Island prison and that the path does not stick more closely to the coast, at least in the vicinity of the prison. Nevertheless, this is a very worthwhile expedition.

Start:	Car park above Beauport
Map Reference:	577482
Bus:	Nos 12, 14 to St. Brelade's Bay, follow the lane to Beauport via St. Brelade's Church
Parking:	Car park above Beauport
Distance:	3 kilometres

Standing above Beauport, with your back to the car park, bear right along the cliff-top footpath. You will enjoy some stunning views from this rocky promontory before emerging into a field.

View down to Beauport

60

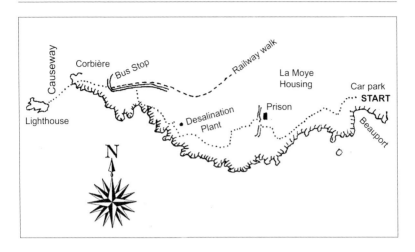

Follow the beaten track along the field edge with the stone wall on your left. Take the left fork at the field corner following the rough stone wall towards the big house ahead. Just before the house bear left, away from the field, towards the sea.

Follow the winding path through a mat of brambles, bracken and gorse – the newish houses of La Moye are in view to the right, as is the boundary fence of Jersey prison.

As you approach the prison the path diverts to the right following the boundary wall of the house. Head along the metalled track about 25 metres ahead to the left. You are now heading towards the white dome (a meteorological radar station) and, beyond it, the desalination plant. Once past the dome look out for a signpost indicating a Public Bridleway. Take the route to the left and follow the beaten path towards the desalination plant and German tower at Corbière.

Follow the cliff-top path down towards the granite structure on the rock below by the track lines. Now ascend the stony path beside the track towards a red gate, then bear left to some steps. At the top of the steps you will see a Public Footpath post – bear left. You now head inland, through the gorse, to reach the road. Cross over and head in the same direction for a further 20 metres to reach the Railway Walk (see Walk 17). Bear left to reach the headland above Corbière.

PORTELET COMMON CIRCULAR

This is a short but invigorating walk up from Ouaisné Bay and promontory which separates Portelet Bay from St. Brelade's Bay. It is common land, around the 200 feet contour, and offers terrific views in every direction. The wild, rocky, largely inaccessible and therefore completely unspoilt coastline to the south-west is really superb.

Start:	Slipway at Ouaisné Bay
Map Reference:	595476
Bus:	No. 12 to turn-offfor Ouaisné
Parking:	Car park at access point to Portelet Common
Distance:	2- 3 kilometres

The walk begins from the slipway at Ouaisné. Cross the beach to the left to reach a signposted Public Footpath at steps at the end of the wall. Climb the steps through an old quarry to emerge on the plateau at Portelet Common.

The view to the north reveals the majestic sweep of St. Brelade's Bay, bisected near its centre by the rocky outcrop known as Le Grouin; before this point the bay is known as Ouaisné, a Martello tower guarding the low, open common behind the sea wall.

Carry on towards the post box of the bungalow which clings, like a bird in a storm, to the rocky outcrop ahead. The wind pump generates power and the barrels collect rainwater. This is 'The Good Life' Jersey-style, and a very romantic vision it presents.

The path now bears left in a southerly direction to take in bracken-covered cliffs which plunge steeply to the rocky foreshore. This is wild coastal scenery but its character is quite

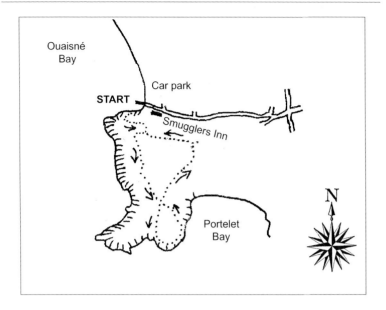

different to that of the north coast. The sea is generally quiet here, the breezes more moderate – you are usually more likely to notice the sound of bird song than the crash of waves and the howl of the wind. The rock here, too, is different, possessing a marked reddish hue. That redness, together with the bright bracken-green slopes (at least in summer) and clear blue sea presents an unforgettable picture.

You eventually reach a stone-built wall at right angles to the cliff edge where you must divert inland by following the wall. Spare a moment to take in the view westwards – you can see beyond St. Brelade's to the diminutive Beauport with its sandy beach and rocky stack rising up at the centre.

Follow the wall towards an old iron gate. It is now permitted to enter the gate and it is well worth doing so in order to make a circuit of this unspoilt headland with its dizzying views down to the sea at Portelet and across the bay towards Noirmont.

Back at the gate and further along the path changes character completely – it is now wooded, mainly with evergreen oaks, and stays this way until you reach the car park at the road entrance/ exit to Portelet Common, when the trees give way to a dense mat

• of gorse and brambles. Follow the track but DO BE CAREFUL.
• The north-facing slope has been quarried in the past and much
• of the path here is sited directly above a sheer drop.

Ouaisné (pronounced 'Way-Nay') is the name given to the southern end of St. Brelade's Bay between the minor promontory of Le Grouin and the rocky headland. It is a good place for swimming, with firm sand which shelves gently at all states of the tide, and is never as crowded as St. Brelade's. Ouaisné Cornmon is a protected area of low-lying land behind the sea wall. There are a number of ponds which take some seeking out amongst the thick undergrowth. A constant battle is fought to restrict the spread of the more rank sort of vegetation, such as gorse and brambles, in order to encourage a varied flora and fauna.

La Cotte de St. Brelade is a west-facing cave situated just below Portelet Common and is a prehistoric site of major importance. Excavation work has been carried out here by the Department of Archaeology and Anthropology of the University of Cambridge since 1960. It has been established that this cave gave shelter to hunting parties between about 150,000 and 100,000 B.C. (middle Palaeolithic). Layers of wind blown soil, clay and rubble have been found to contain rich remains of food and flint tools (originating from the mainland before rising sea levels cut off the supply), making La Cotte de St. Brelade one of the most important middle Palaeolithic sites in Europe.

NOIRMONT CIRCULAR

This is a pleasant walk to the Noirmont promontory, familiar to sea-borne visitors to the island, and most heavily fortified by the Germans who were aware of its strategic position looking out over the flat expanse of St. Aubin's Bay and the approaches to St. Helier's harbour.

Start:	Noirmont car park or 'START' on map if bus-bound
Map Reference:	606466 or 604476
Bus:	No. 12 to stop for Noirmont
Parking:	At Noirmont Point itself, in which case join this route at point 'S' – see map.
Distance:	3 Kilometres

Ramblers who approach Noirmont by the Portelet bus should alight at the crossroads about a quarter of a mile before the terminus – ask the driver for the Ouaisné turning. At this crossroads (facing south), lanes lead left to Belcroute, right to Ouaisné and straight on for Noirmont.

Just beyond the crossroads is a signposted Footpath and Bridleway on the left. This leads you through a clump of trees and continues along the boundary of Noirmont Manor, defined by a high chain-link fence which may be unpicturesque but at least has the virtue of offering a view through it, over the wooded coastal slopes and across St. Aubin's Bay.

The path opens up as you approach Noirmont – here is an alternative lower path which descends beneath the rocky promontory capped by its huge gun emplacement. For once there really is a gun emplaced here – a weapon recovered in 1979 from the bottom of the cliffs at Les Landes in the north-west corner of

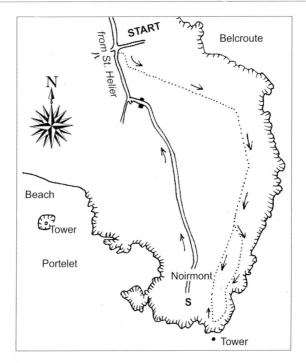

- the island where the liberating forces, with a fine disdain for their
- tourist potential, dumped numerous bits of German hardware
- (see drawing on Page 120).
-   This descending path leads you down to face the Martello
- tower which is set on a seaward rock. From here you can scramble
- up the rock face (not too demanding) and this will bring you out
- amid the complex of fortifications. To the west you can look down
- to Portelet Bay with its sandy beach and isthmus linking L'Ile au
- Guerdain, complete with tower.

German Fortifications: No visitor to Jersey can fail to notice the
defences built by the occupying Germans between 1940 and 1945.
The contrast between grey cement and the native rocks makes them
even more noticeable than the Martello towers, sea walls and
slipways of an earlier period. The west and south coasts in particular,
which the Germans regarded as the most likely to be attacked by
the British, are extremely heavily fortified.

The German Occupation is a dark chapter in the history of the islands and, following the Liberation, all attempts were made to obliterate, as far as possible, the legacy of those years, though the concrete structures themselves will endure for many centuries. I don't remember Jersey before the Occupation and it is difficult to imagine Noirmont and similar strategic promontories without the presence of towers and gun emplacements. They serve as a permanent reminder of the ruthlessness and utter folly of one nation attempting to dominate others by brute force. They are also monuments to the suffering of thousands of slave workers, kept in appalling conditions, who laboured on these enormous structures of reinforced concrete. The English never invaded, of course, so Hitler's Channel Island defences were never tested. When Normandy fell to the Allies, the occupying Germans were cut off for many months and themselves suffered hardships.

Fortifications at Noirmont

Portelet Bay: Unlike Beauport on the far side of St. Brelade's, is well built up with hotels and apartments. A long staircase leads down to the sandy beach which, according to the tide, connects with a rocky islet known as the Ile au Guerdain, topped with a Martello tower. Before this, the island had been the burial place of one Philippe Janvrin, a sea captain who, in 1721, whilst confined to his ship at Belcroute, died of the plague. His body was not allowed to be brought ashore and was buried on the Ile so that the rock is often referred to as Janvrin's Tomb.

THE RAILWAY WALK

via Quennevais to Corbière

This walk follows the course of the former Jersey Railway, on its route from St. Aubin to Corbière. It therefore has no steep inclines, though there is a noticeable rise from St. Aubin to Quennevais, and a lesser slope from Quennevais to Corbière.

Start: St. Aubin village
Map Reference: 606488
Bus: Nos. 12, 14, 15 to St. Aubin
Parking: On road or quay at St. Aubin
Distance: 6 kilometres

The entrance to the **Railway Walk** is found on the left of the main road just as it turns inland from **St. Aubin's Harbour**. This route needs absolutely no description for the purpose of direction finding – you simply follow the track until you reach the end of the line, or however far you wish to go. The path is well maintained; there is lots of interest in the vegetation which grows on either side, with the scene constantly changing.

The 'new town' of **Quennevais** is the half-way point. Here the track passes under the road, just before which there is a large playground which might provide a respite for the children. If you wish you can climb up to the road at the bridge and bear south (left) to find shops and a pub.

The second half of the walk is somewhat different in character. The path is bordered mainly by pines (though much has had to be replanted following the 1987 Hurricane); the soil is blown sand from St. Ouen's and the grit path is dappled with sunlight which

St. Aubin harbour entrance left high and dry at low tide, one of the reasons it was overtaken by the newer harbour at St. Helier, opened in 1846.

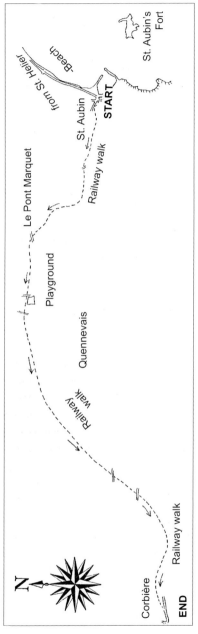

penetrates the overarching trees. this is a delightful part of the walk and, if you have children accompanying you, they might just be convinced that this is the real Yellow Brick Road (perhaps, more accurately, the 'Yellow Grit Road'). I cannot guarantee that they will see the Scarecrow and the Tin Man but I fancy I did when I was a child walking along here. The railway ended above Corbière, just before the road is reached. The station building is now a private house, but the platform beside the track is obvious. If you look hard enough in the vicinity of the terminus, you will doubtless find sections of iron rail stuck in the ground. The lighthouse can be reached by a causeway when the tide is low but do heed the bell which warns of the incoming tide.

Alternative mini-circular walk from the Railway Walk near St. Aubin's: Not very far from the start of the Railway Walk at St. Aubin's, behind the backs of the buildings along the road, you will find some steps in the slope on your left leading to an ascending path. This will lead you to a viewpoint above St. Aubin's town, far from the hurly-burly, but with a great view over the harbour to St. Aubin's

Fort and beyond. It is a worthwhile diversion from the main track.

The Railway Walk follows the course of the old railway which ran from St. Helier along the sea wall to St. Aubin, and thence to Corbière. The line opened to St. Aubin in 1870 and was extended to Corbière in 1899. It had a chequered history of financial failures and takeovers; the number of passengers peaked in the mid-twenties and thereafter went into decline, until motor transport and a disastrous fire at St. Aubin's Station caused its eventual demise a decade later. St. Aubin's Station and Hotel, a fine building, now houses St. Brelade's Parish Hall, whilst the St. Helier terminus is Tourism headquarters. Walking between St. Aubin and Corbière you will encounter a number of bridges crossing the track whose style betrays their railway origin. The former station at the Corbière terminus is self-evident.

St. Aubin is one of my favourite bits of 'old Jersey'. The town was Jersey's premier trading port before St. Helier's harbour was built in the last century. Its former importance and prosperity is reflected in the many former merchants' houses, dating mainly from the seventeenth and eighteenth centuries, which stand near the harbour.

The walk to the ends of each protective arm of the harbour is always pleasant, not just for the immediate interest of the boats in dock, but also for the prospect of St. Aubin's Fort offshore. There is a wealth of picturesque backwaters to explore in this diminutive town built against the steep hillside. Market Street climbs up from the harbour and narrow stairways reach back down. In the opposite direction, behind the coast road, there is High Street, used only by local traffic now but which, before the coast road was extended in the last century to link La Haule and St. Aubin, served as the main road. High Street is chock full of handsome old houses, sometimes with courtyards and steps and glimpses of the widening view across the bay.

BEAUMONT CIRCULAR

via Sandybrook, Tesson Mill, Le Moulin de Quetivel and Jersey War Tunnels

This is a varied walk which includes a surviving fragment of sanctuary path, together with short stretches of path which have relatively recently been opened up along the beautiful St. Peter's Valley. The route passes Le Moulin de Quetivel, an ancient water mill which has been restored to full working condition and within view of the Jersey War Tunnels.

Start:	From 'Seaside' bus stop – one before Beaumont
Map Reference:	616498
Bus:	Nos. 9, 12, 14, 15 to 'Seaside'
Parking:	Car park between road and promenade at 'Seaside'
Distance:	4 kilometres, but feels longer

Alight from the bus at the stop before **Beaumont** (known as 'Seaside'). To begin the walk make for the pedestrian crossing near the bus stop on the St. Helier side of Beaumont junction. Cross the road here and go straight on by the wide gravelly track – the Perquage, or sanctuary path – which heads directly inland across the flat, low-lying Le Marais de St. Pierre, a former marsh. This is a pleasant walk between cultivated fields. At the end of this path we reach the small community known as **Sandybrook**, with its shops and the **Sanctuary Café**.

Turn left and then right up **Rue du Moulin** – the three-storey blocks of flats on the right are known as **Perquage Court**. You

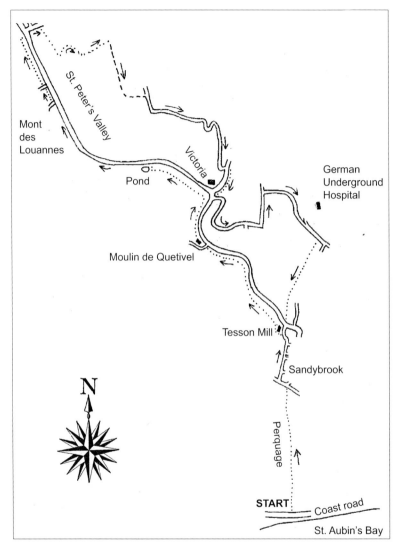

soon reach a pleasant green with a flowing stream and the impressive bulk of Tesson Mill. Just before the old mill building look out for a lane rising to the left and heralded by a Jersey National Trust sign indicating 'Footpath to Rough Tor'. Soon you can look down on the remains of the overshot water-wheel at the rear of Tesson Mill and the mill stream cascading uselessly to

Above: Tesson Mill, acquired by the Jersey National Trust in 1996;

Below: Approach to pond in St. Peter's Valley from Le Don Gaudin

the bottom of the wheel and feeding the brook we have been following from the beginning of the walk.

The footpath becomes a dirt track and then reverts to a narrow footpath as we begin to enter St. Peter's Valley. The path follows a course near the edge of a hanging wood on the west side of the valley, just above the mill stream, and gives us views across the valley bottom to the road on the far side. In spring there are bluebells, red campion, white stichwort and comfrey.

You emerge on the road – **Mont Fallu** – opposite the handsome old mill known as **Le Moulin de Quetivel**, restored by the Jersey National Trust. Just behind the mill bear right, climb the granite steps and follow the footpath further up St. Peter's Valley. This is a very pleasant walk through **Le Don Gaudin**, a hanging wood with primroses and violets, which all too soon takes you to the pond and car park (where visitors are encouraged to leave their cars and walk by the footpath to Le Moulin de Quetivel.)

There is a little green area beside the pond which makes an excellent picnic spot. At the end of this green area you will find a footpath fenced off from the field below the road. Follow this safe, pleasant route as far as **Le Mont des Louannes** on the left. Head up here to reach the signposted footpath on the right.

Follow this the short distance to the next lane, **Le Mont du Presbytère**, and cross over to enter a pleasant footpath which runs parallel to the road. This eventually emerges on the road opposite the lane called **Le Mont de L'Ecole**. Head along here for a very short distance until you find the start of a footpath on the right; follow this as it climbs the wooded hillside to reach a wide track.

Bear left and follow the track until you reach a crossing; here turn right towards the farm buildings, then bear left to reach the lane called **La Rue du Panigot** and turn right to head downhill to meet **La Route de L'Aleval**. Cross the road to find the entrance to a little footpath through the woods at the edge of the car park at the junction with St. Peter's Valley. The **Victoria** pub is just to the right.

To continue the walk, turn left up the narrow winding lane signposted **Les Gellettes**. The lane takes a 90° turn to the left at the transport works on the summit. Take the next right down **Le Mont du Rocher** – you will soon see the **Jersey War Tunnels** to your left.

At the junction with the lane called **La Rue des Pres Sorsoleil** you will spot a signposted footpath on the right which leads up through dense woods to a south-facing bluff. This is the third and final climb on this walk and your last chance of a view southwards to St. Aubin's Bay.

Descend the hillside by the footpath on the far side to reach, once again, St. Peter's Valley in the vicinity of **Tesson Mill**. From here you retrace your steps back via **Sandybrook** and the Sanctuary Path to reach **Beaumont**.

The Sanctuary Path or **Perquage**, which we follow at the outset of this walk, is a surviving fragment of the path which connected St. Lawrence Parish Church with the shore near Beaumont. Every parish once possessed its own sanctuary path between its church and a convenient point on the coast. Before the Reformation, suspects could take sanctuary in the Church and then escape the island by taking the sanctuary path, or perquage, to the sea. This illustrates the way in which the authorities encouraged undesirables to deport themselves, a sentiment, if not a method, which survives in the island to this day. It would be wonderful to be able to re-establish all these ancient sanctuary paths today, not for escape but for exploration.

Le Moulin de Quetivel: Now under the auspices of the Jersey National Trust, has a recorded history dating back to 1309 and was brought back into use as a mill during the German Occupation. After a fire in 1969 the Jersey National Trust set about restoring the fabric and installing redundant machinery from other Jersey mills. The old mill stream still carries water to turn the mill wheel and corn is ground into flour, an operation which can be witnessed by visitors in the season.

WATERWORKS VALLEY CIRCULAR 1

● ●

via Mont Felard, St. Lawrence Church and Hamptonne

A longish route, but one well worth following in order to appreciate the fine group of buildings at the centre of St. Lawrence Parish and the sylvan charms of St. Lawrence Valley, more generally known as Waterworks Valley. The route down the valley has been made even more enjoyable to ramblers by the creation of the Sentier des Moulins, an off-road route and millennium project carried out by the parishioners of St Lawrence.

There is a shop and pub opposite St. Lawrence Church. The Hamptonne complex, belonging to the Jersey National Trust, lies beside the route at the half-way point. There are ample opportunities for picnicking in Waterworks Valley.

Start:	Mont Felard – see below
Map Reference:	628498
Bus:	Nos. 7, 8, 9, 12, 14, 15 to Mont Felard
Parking:	Car park at Millbrook Park/ Glass Church
Distance:	8 kilometres

The walk begins at a point on the inner road just to the east (the town side) of **Mont Felard**, between **Les Aumonts** apartment block and the entrance to **Waterworks Valley**. You will find a metalled path leading uphill and signposted **Pedestrians Only**. Follow this track as it climbs between old stone walls and above the recently built flats on the right. You soon reach the road on Mont Felard, here very deeply sunken into the bedrock.

Notice how loose and fragmented the rock is – this is not your Jersey granite but an outcrop of the Jersey Shale Formation of

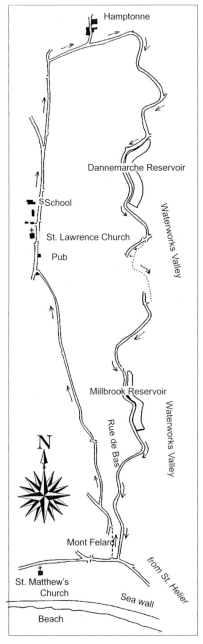

which the centre and middle-west of the island largely consists. Fortunately, you have to negotiate this busy road for not more than a hundred metres when you bear right along **Rue de Bas**. This minor lane is followed for about a one and a half kilometres – a somewhat uneventful way which at least has the virtue of peace and quiet – until you reach the main road once more at **Strudels Tea Rooms** where you bear right. Immediately the stately bulk of **St. Lawrence Church**, like a great ship sailing in from the west, comes into view.

Follow the main road on the right until you reach a fork at **Mont Felard Garage**: here you bear right along **Rue des Corvées** – notice the commemorative stone erected by parishioners in 1985 to mark the fortieth anniversary of the Liberation. Follow the lane and bear right at Inverness Lodge where you begin to descend towards Water-works Valley.

On the left is **Rue de la Patente**, which gives access to the **Hamptonne** Country Life Museum. Keep descending past the meadow on the left, along the centre of which flows a stream which eventually joins the larger stream flowing southwards in Waterworks Valley itself.

As the lane bears right, look out for the footpath sign on the left. Enter the field and bear right to follow the path beside the stone wall. Cross a wooden footbridge over a stream, bear right, cross the road and descend wooden steps to follow the stream-side path. Look out for a sign which indicates a way back across the stream to the right. Follow this undulating path close to the foot of a wooded slope and emerge onto the road through hewn rocks.

Turn right at the road and look out for a footpath sign near the head of Dannemarche Reservoir. Climb the wooden steps and enjoy a high-level walk looking down through the trees to the water. Descend a flight of 74 steps to cross a track; follow the path opposite as it descends to follow a stream. Look out for a footpath sign near a metal gate and bear right as indicated. Negotiate wooden stepping stones and a footbridge autographed with staples and continue by a fenced path along the edge of a boggy field.

Emerge on to the road, bear left and right and look out for a footpath sign by the stone engraved 'Vicart'. After a climb of 50 metres bear right (see signpost). You may catch a glimpse of the St Lawrence Millennium Standing Stone to the right. Descend and follow the path beside the millstream. Ignore a couple of left turnings and continue down the valley to eventually cross the millstream where you follow the fenced path across a footbridge to join the road.

Carry on until the recent, brick-built flats on the right – **Le Clos de Petit Felard** – mark the end of Waterworks Valley and the approach of the main road.

St. Lawrence: Opposite the church is a shop and pub (St. Lawrence Stores and the British Union respectively) whilst, just past it is the Parish Hall, a building of considerable grandeur erected in 1882. Following this is St. Lawrence Arsenal and then the Elementary School, dated 1902. All these edifices – the church, the parish room, the arsenal and the school – are built of the same pink granite, which only adds to their attractiveness.

St. Lawrence Arsenal – note the cannon balls on top of the building on the right.

Hamptonne is a complex of traditional Jersey farm buildings which have been acquired by the Island's Museum Service and restored to their former appearance. In the season it is possible to catch a special bus from the Museum in St. Helier to reach Hamptonne. However you reach this somewhat hidden-away site in the centre of the Island you should not miss a chance to visit. There is an enlightening display on various aspects of Jersey farming life, attractive gardens and orchard, various special interest displays, and an excellent cafe which offers some traditional Jersey dishes and a relaxing atmosphere.

WATERWORKS VALLEY CIRCULAR 2

via Mont Cochon, Fern Valley and Mont à l'Abbe

This walk uses a mixture of Green Lanes and footpaths which are, surprisingly, almost all within the parish of St. Helier. Fern valley is a delightfully unspoilt spot. There are two climbs – first up Mont Cochon, then out of Fern Valley and up towards St. John's Road.

Start:	Mouth of Waterworks Valley
Map Reference:	631501
Bus:	Nos 7, 8, 9, 12, 14, 15 to Millbrook
Parking:	Limited on-road parking at mouth of Waterworks Valley
Distance:	4-5 kilometres

Begin the walk by heading up the quiet and peaceful **Waterworks Valley**, past **Millbrook Reservoir** (constructed 1895/6) as far as the little lane signposted **Ruelle de St. Clair**. Turn into this lane as far as the sharp leftward bend. Here you bear right by the footpath in front of **Lakeside Cottage**. The reservoir is now to your right with the old mill stream between the footpath and reservoir.

The path climbs the hillside and soon bifurcates – keep bearing left to follow a narrow way between a field to the right and a hedgebank on the left. Notice the view south towards the mouth of Waterworks Valley and the expanse of St. Aubin's Bay. At the head of the valley here head along the sunken lane until you reach the B-road on Mont Cochon.

Turn left, pass **Ruelle de St. Clair** on the left and, opposite, right into Fern Valley. **Fern Valley** is a designated Green Lane and you will find it very quiet as you descend to the valley bottom.

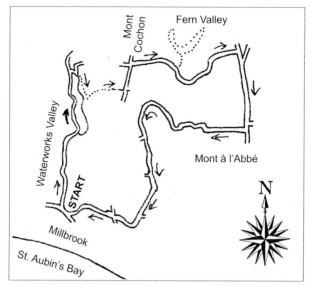

Here you will spot a Jersey National Trust sign indicating access to a footpath which explores a circuit of two little connecting valleys just upstream and is a very worthwhile detour, the path crossing streams by stepping stones and traversing wooded slopes above open meadow.

After this natural break, continue along the lane as it winds up the hillside. Turn right at the T-junction and head south via **La Grande Route du Mont à l'Abbé** until you reach **Rue Fliquet** on the right.

Turn down this sharply winding lane to descend to the valley bottom where you bear right and then sharp left up **La Ruelle Vaucluse**. As you reach the summit notice the prominent red and white painted chimney of the incinerator at Bellozanne to the left.

As the lane swings right you have a brief view across St. Aubin's Bay but the lane becomes so sunken beneath the fields on either side that visibility is somewhat restricted. Eventually you reach houses on the left and **Mont Cochon**. Cross over and continue in the same direction via **Rue de Trachy**, until you reach the main road, pass the Millbrook lavoir and your starting point.

Lavoir at Millbrook

The North Coast Path

Undoubtedly the jewel in the crown of Jersey's network of footpaths, the North Coast Path is well signposted, well maintained, safe and easily accessible from any number of bus stops and car parks and leads the walker to the Island's truly formidable north coast. It seems extraordinary to reflect that much of this footpath is of quite recent origin; much of it was surveyed in the 1980s and subsequently constructed as winter work by the island's prison population.

Unfortunately, there are still a few gaps. As we have already noted at the end of Walk 6, there is no coast path between Fliquet and La Coupe, Jersey's north-easterly promontory, the point at which the north coast could logically be said to begin. Between the remote headland at La Coupe and the charming wooded cove about half a mile west there exists an unofficial path which is more a scramble than a ramble. Because of its inaccessibility and its difficulty I have not described it here.

The North Coast Path proper begins behind Rozel, though there is a stretch of the coast here which is bypassed. The path is happily then complete all the way to the north-west corner, with the exception of a mile or two in the west of St. John's Parish where the path joins La Route du Nord which at first closely follows the cliff-top and then diverts inland slightly in order to bypass a coastal rubbish tip at La Saline and the great quarry at Ronez. The North Coast Path is one of the Great Jersey Experiences.

The North Coast Path is here described in 6 sections, each between 4 and 6 kilometres – Walks 21, 23, 26, 28, 30 and 31, Alternatively, a number of circular walks are described, each of which includes a section of the Coast Path – Walks 22, 24, 25, 27 and 29.

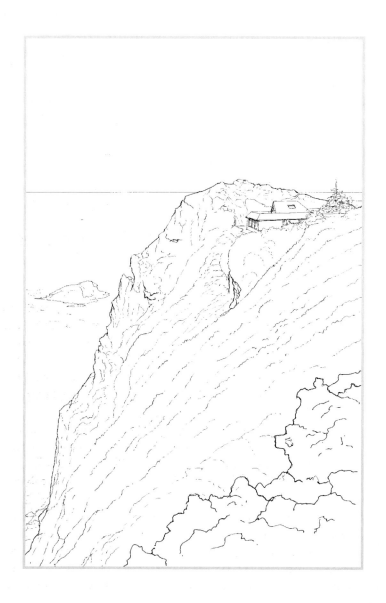

ROZEL - BOULEY BAY

This portion of the North Coast Path is fairly undulating though no prolonged steep climbs are encountered. There are facilities for eating and drinking at both ends.

Start:	Rozel Bay
Map Reference:	696544
Bus:	No.3 to Rozel No.21 from Bouley Bay (in summer)
Parking:	Parking is fairly restricted at Rozel, being mainly on the roadside.
Distance:	4 kilometres

Follow the main road at the back of Rozel; before the road bears uphill to the left you bear right along the lane signposted **White Rock and Cliff Path**. Follow this rising lane until it gradually levels out. Immediately past the complex of farmbuildings which straddles the lane you turn right and follow the track – you will see a sign on the wall of the building indicating **Parking, Footpath, Cliff Walk to White Rock**.

Follow the track until you reach the car park with its view in a north-easterly direction, and continue by the coast path which can be found at the far end of the car park. The path is around the 200 foot contour and looks down onto the rocky, indented coastline.

Eventually you will reach a stone marker indicating **Rozel: one and a half miles**; Bouley Bay is half a mile further. In front of you is a portion of land which appears to be rather detached from the general plateau; this area is known as **Le Jardin d'Olivet**. Drop down to cross the stream and climb again along the seaward

flank of Le Jardin. This is common land and there is a maze of paths criss-crossing its verdant expanse.

Simply follow the main path above the shore and continue until you reach **Bouley Bay**, via the grounds of the **Bouley Bay Hotel**.

Rozel is a cove backed by high wooded hillsides and faces the north-east. The sea wall leads past cafés and restaurants to a small quay which affords protection for a number of fishing boats. The bay is generally rocky and is not the best place to enjoy a swim. If you walk up the main road out of Rozel it is possible to bear left by an unmade track – **Rue des Fontanelles** – which is signposted as a footpath, and to descend through hanging woods to reach another of Jersey's famous dolmens, this one known as Le Couperon. The upright stones define a passage 27 feet long and support seven massive capstones, the whole surrounded by an outer wall.

Above: Ropes and geese, Rozel Harbour;

Below: Sign, La Tête des Hougues

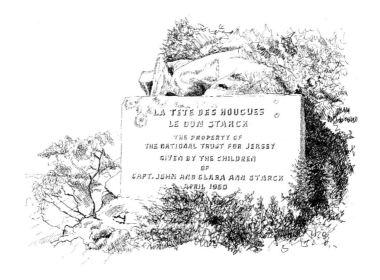

BOULEY BAY CIRCULAR

*Bouley Bay via North Coast Path, Trinity village and
Le Grand Côtil du Boulay.*

This walk offers an attractive combination of coast and country. The climbing is in the first half of the walk. After Trinity village, with its church and pub, it's downhill all the way. Refreshments available at Bouley Bay and Trinity village.

Start:	Bouley Bay
Map Reference:	669547
Bus:	No. 21 (in summer only)
Parking:	Car park above Bouley Bay
Distance:	5 Kilometres

To begin the walk you need to locate the continuation of the North Coast Path in a westerly direction from Bouley Bay. This is clearly signposted – **To Bonne Nuit** – beside the road just above the bay. The course of the path is described in Walk 20, though from a direction-finding viewpoint, it really needs no description as it is all perfectly straightforward, and always a beautiful route.

After about two kilometres the path forsakes the cliff-top and enters some wooded slopes which hang above a valley. There is a maze of paths here and it is easy to become lost, particularly as the signposts are often vandalised. At the first cross-track, marked by a small clearing featuring a mature beech tree, bear right to follow the coast path. Descend the path but keep a look out for a path bearing sharply away to the left, a few yards above the stream in the valley bottom. (If you reach a stone indicating **Footpath to Bonne Nuit** you will know you have gone too far

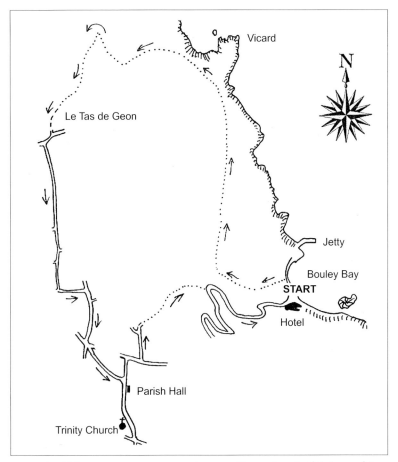

and will have to retrace your steps until you locate this branching path which heads up the valley).

Follow the rough path up through the woods. If you stick to the most well beaten path you should have no problem, and you will eventually reach a wooden fence and a Jersey National Trust sign announcing this as **Le Don Averty**. Pass through the gateposts and continue by the path, climbing a little with each step.

When you emerge at the road you turn right and then sharp left along **La Rue de Cambrai**. Carry on until you reach the houses at the crossroads and bear left – notice the dovecote in the gable of the house on the right.

Turn right at the T-junction and carry on until you reach the junction with the main road, marked by an impressive monument to **Phillippe Le Vesconte**, a former Constable of the Parish. On the right is a general store. To continue the walk: bear left, via the main road, which has a pavement on the left. This will lead you to the Parish Hall and Church. You emerge at a T-junction with the **Parish Hall** opposite. **Holy Trinity Church** occupies a commanding position at a road junction to the right and you may wish to visit the church, if not the Trinity Arms pub on the far side of the main road to the left.

Walk back past the Parish Hall and turn right at the T-junction, then left after a short distance down the lane signposted **La Rue des Fontaines**. At the point where the lane bears left make for the footpath just to the left of the entrance drive to **La Brunerie** directly in front of you. This is in the form of a boundary path hemmed in by a high hedge on the left and the boundary wall of the property on the right.

You descend the path until you reach a cross track. Immediately on the left is a dilapidated *lavoir,* where a natural spring trickles forth, and a well next to it. On the right is the entrance to Jersey National Trust land signposted **Le Grand Côtil de Boulay**. Follow the path as it descends quite steeply through woods with a tiny stream beside it until you eventually join the lane which winds down to Bouley Bay.

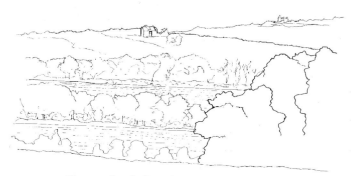

Hut on the skyline, from Rue de Cambrai

Trinity Church is sited in the centre of the parish on a crossroads though this could not fairly be described as a village centre. There is a pub, and the parish hall and shop are not far away but the houses are well scattered. Trinity is a large parish whose coastline begins at Rozel and stretches all the way to Giffard Bay, adjacent to Bonne Nuit, and which boasts Jersey's highest point at Les Platons: 534 feet above sea level, and has earned it the dubious honour of being encrusted with a plethora of electronic masts.

Lavoir: Examples of this characteristic piece of Jersey street furniture can be seen throughout the island. They were constructed beside springs or along stream courses and utilised the water source to provide a place for the washing of clothes and linen. Such is the structure beside the track just before the entrance to Le Grand Côtil du Boulay, though adjoining it there is an iron-gated wellhead.

The coast at Vicard

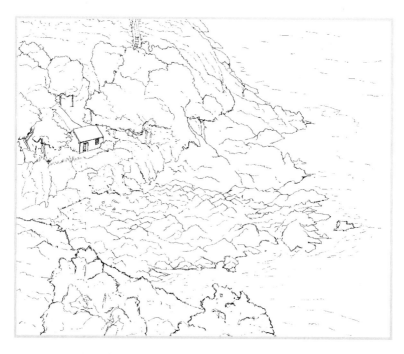

Wolf's Lair

BOULEY BAY - BONNE NUIT

To my mind, the next few kilometres constitute the most beautiful and exhilarating section of the entire North Coast Path. Refreshment available at either end.

Start:	Bouley Bay
Map Reference:	669547
Bus:	No.21 to Bouley Bay, No. 4 from Bonne Nuit
Parking:	Car park above Bouley Bay
Distance:	7 kilometres

Walking out of Bouley Bay, look out for a signpost indicating the cliff path to **Bonne Nuit** as 4 miles. To begin this section of the walk there is a very steep climb by steps out of the bay. At first, the path diverts to the landward side of the massif up which you have just toiled, and there are fine long views back into the hinterland of Trinity Parish. Eventually the path enters woodland where there is a crossing of ways. You bear right and follow the stream down to the sea where you bear to the left of the hut named **Wolf's Lair**. Notice the tablet here which commemorates a French/British commando raid in 1943.

The next section of coast path is completely unspoilt and quite outstanding. The hillside sweeping down to the sea which the path traverses is covered in heather and bracken and beside the path, in spring, grow white campion, bluebells, spurge, primroses, with pennywort on rocky outcrops. You climb the next promontory and gain views westwards over the sister bays of **Le Havre Giffard** and **Bonne Nuit**, and past these to the granite workings at **Ronez**.

The path now forks and you have a choice of an Upper or a

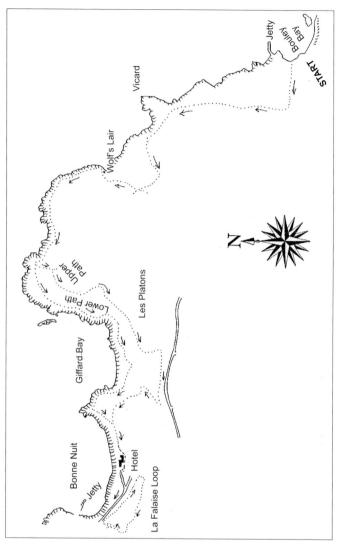

Lower Path. The latter is rather more direct and less wearisome and obviously nearer the sea. The upper path leads you through much heather and you may find yourself humming "I'll tak' the high road ..." The twin paths reunite on the east side of Bonne Nuit and you eventually join the road to reach the jetty and hotel on the west side of the bay.

L'Etacquerel Fort

Bouley Bay is one of the north coast's larger inlets and a natural harbour. Its vulnerability so close to France called for defences: L'Etacquerel Fort at the east end of the bay (this can be viewed more closely in Walk 21) dates from the early nineteenth century. The peace and quiet along the lane which leads up the steep wooded hillside to around the 400 feet contour is shattered annually during the Bouley Bay Hill Climb when cars and motorcycles struggle to reach the summit first.

Walk 24

LA VALLETTE LOOP

A short circular walk on the steep hillside above Bonne Nuit.
(A map seems superfluous accompaniment in this instance and has
been omitted).

Start:	Bonne Nuit Bay
Map Reference:	640559
Bus:	No.4 to Bonne Nuit
Parking:	Car park at Bonne Nuit
Distance:	1 kilometre

Beside the lane which descends to Bonne Nuit from the south-east, on the left, you will notice a Jersey National Trust signpost indicating the start of **La Vallette Walk**. This is in the form of a loop on the craggy hillside above, and can obviously be tackled in a clockwise or an anti-clockwise fashion; I favour the former.

If you agree, bear left and begin the climb, at first fairly gentle but later more steep. At the top of the slope the footpath bends right to follow the field boundary on your left and eventually bears right again to descend the steep hillside by a series of hairpin bends. This walk may seem slightly pointless but sitting down to a picnic at the summit of the hillside will invest it with more meaning and afford you ample opportunity to take in the view over Bonne Nuit.

BONNE NUIT CIRCULAR

*via North Coast Path, L'Auberge du Nord and
St. John's VIllage*

This walk, taking in a section of the North Coast Path, gives us a taste of St. John's, one of Jersey's northern parishes, and passes one of my favourite pubs, L'Auberge du Nord, a genuinely ancient hostelry unspoilt by the demands of the present day – a great place to visit on a cold winter's day with a log fire blazing beside the bar.

Start:	Bonne Nuit Bay
Map Reference:	640559
Bus:	No.4 to Bonne Nuit
Parking:	Car park at Bonne Nuit
Distance:	1 kilometre

From Bonne Nuit you begin by finding the continuation of the North Coast Path in a westerly direction. Like Bouley Bay, there is a stiff climb to begin with, followed by an exhilarating cliff-top walk past **Wolf 's Caves** – the modern pub stands beside the path, the caves are a steep climb down the cliff face – and on to La Saline rubbish dump, not the choicest spot on the North Coast Path.

When you reach the metalled road you turn right to follow **La Route du Nord** which from here to Sorel serves as the North Coast Path. At the next junction bear left, directly inland, towards St. John's village, but via **L'Auberge du Nord**, the old pub on the right. From **St. John's Church** and village centre, with your back to the main road running east-west, bear right by the lane between the shops, namely **The Pharmacy** on the left and **Central Stores** on the right. Follow this lane until you leave the village behind. When you reach the road junction turn left to follow the lane as it twists and turns and descends to Bonne Nuit.

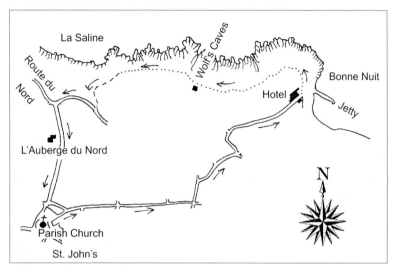

Bonne Nuit: 'Good Night' Bay is a typical north coast inlet, with a mainly rocky foreshore, a small quay to protect its fishing boats, many of which are employed in lobster fishing, and backed by steep hills. The rock, known as Le Cheval Guillaume, in the centre of the bay, was for many years the site of a pagan pilgrimage enacted every midsummer day when folk would wait to be rowed round the rock to avoid bad luck in the coming year. Apparently such a custom still survives in the Orkneys and Shetlands! Like Bouley Bay, Bonne Nuit's defences were constantly being strengthened prior to the mid-nineteenth century.

Old Jersey apple crusher

BONNE NUIT - DEVIL'S HOLE

A fairly deserted section of the north coast path; refreshments available at both ends (in the season).

Start: Bonne Nuit Bay
Map Reference: 640560
Bus: No.4 to Bonne Nuit, No. 7 from Devil's Hole
Parking: Car park at Bonne Nuit
Distance: 6 kilometres

Just above the **Bonne Nuit Hotel**, on the right hand side of the lane, look out for a signpost indicating the coast path to **La Saline**. The start of this section is quite a steep haul though perhaps not as taxing as the climb out of Bouley Bay (Walk 23). At the top you can look back over Bonne Nuit Bay and the circular La Vallette Walk (Walk 24) which is hacked out of the hillside behind the bay.

You will soon be enjoying great coastal scenery as promontory follows promontory and the cliffs tumble precipitously to the shore. The path skirts the eponymous pub, **Wolf's Caves**, which stands 400 feet above the caves themselves. Follow the path to La Saline which is, disappointingly, a rubbish shoot. You ascend the drive to reach **La Route du Nord**. You can turn left here to reach St. John's village (see the spire of St. John's Church due south) and, more immediately, the pub known as **L'Auberge du Nord** (highly recommended).

To continue the walk, bear right and follow the well laid La Route du Nord (early 1940s), and head past the Ronez quarry complex. At Sorel Farm turn right to regain the coast path.

You go straight ahead to the cul de sac and headland at Sorel

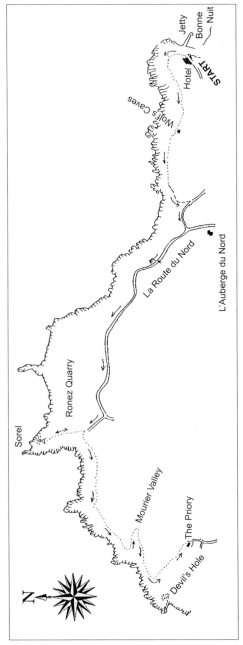

with its car park and great views.

Retrace your steps towards **Sorel Farm** and, beside **St. John Millennium Standing Stone,** continue westwards by the coast path until you reach Mourier Valley where the path heads sharply inland and downhill to reach the footbridge which takes the footpath to the far side. Quite soon, you must head inland once again, this time towards the group of buildings at the head of Devil's Hole, including the **Priory pub**. You go straight ahead to the cul de sac and headland at Sorel with its car park and great views.

La Route du Nord is a fine road from St. John's to Sorel which was constructed during the German Occupation by some of the many local men, who were otherwise unemployed.

Sorel is the northernmost tip of Jersey and a favourite viewpoint.

Directly north lies Sark and, between the two islands, the rocky reef known as the Paternosters, so called because so many ships came to grief on them, and sailors were in the habit of saying their prayers as they passed: 'Pater Noster' = 'Our Father'.

Above: At Sorel Point; Below: Recycled fortification, Sorel

Devil's Hole, with a wrecked staircase which formerly gave access to the diabolical depths.

DEVIL'S HOLE CIRCULAR

via Tombette, Mourier Valley and North Coast Path

The Mourier Valley has a timeless feel, perhaps owing to the presence of a number of old unimproved properties, which lends a charming quality to the gentle, green valley dipping inevitably towards the sea, the lower section of which forms the boundary between the parishes of St. John's and St. Mary's.

Start:	The Priory, Devil's Hole
Map Reference:	607558
Bus:	No.7 to Devil's Hole
Parking:	Car park at Devil's Hole – but note that this is not a public car park
Distance:	3 kilometres

From Devil's Hole, where there is a good pub – The Priory – follow the lane inland (ignoring the signposted cliff path to Grève de Lecq) past Jersey's own vineyard but not as far as the Butterfly Farm. Turn into the first lane on the left. At the next small crossroads, **Haut Tombette** is indicated along the lane to the right. Turn left here and follow the lane to reach a crossroads at **L'Ecluse** where you bear left towards the Mourier Valley. You will overhear a chuckling stream to the right of the lane.

At the house called **Les Hougues**, take the right fork along a rough track; this eventually leads past a small reservoir into which the stream flows. Cross the wooden footbridge, over the stream and join the coast path as it skirts the steep hillside sloping to the sea and rises gradually to a promontory above the great cleft at Devil's Hole. Turn left here to reach the pub, bus terminus and car park.

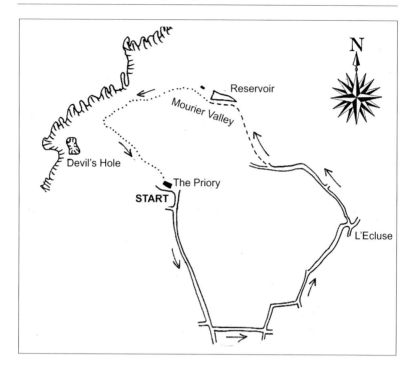

Devil's Hole is the rather gruesome appellation given to a natural blow hole and is properly known as Le Creux de Vis (= 'screw hole'). A cave has been invaded by the sea which, over the years, has blown a hole in its roof through to the sky above. Some curious impulse led someone to place an effigy of the devil in the hole.

Mourier Valley carries a stream which drains the eastern part of St. Mary's Parish, which has a decidedly remote, even deserted atmosphere, enjoyed to its full in this walk. Indeed, the stream once drove three water mills; now the small pumping station diverts the stream into Waterworks Valley to the south.

The coast from Devil's Hole

Towards Devil's Hole from the west.

DEVIL'S HOLE - GREVE DE LECQ

· ·

This portion of the North Coast Path is a favourite of mine. The mile and a half or so between Devil's Hole and Crabbé is most dramatic – ferocious cliffs where the sea has excavated deep inlets and numerous caves. The whole of this section is within the quiet agricultural parish of St. Mary's and, indeed, fields are your only view inland.

Start:	The Priory, Devil's Hole
Map Reference:	607558
Bus:	No. 7 to Devil's Hole, Nos. 7B, 9 from Grève de Lecq
Parking:	Car park at Devil's Hole – but note that this is not a public car park.
Distance:	4 kilometres

From the **Priory pub** at Devil's Hole head back up the lane until you see the sign indicating '**Cliff Path to Greve de Lecq 2 and a half miles**' where you turn right. Soon you will see another signpost directing you rightwards, and the track becomes a coast path proper. Simply follow the well defined path along its course between the fields and the cliffs.

At the first promontory, **Le Col de la Rocque** (note the Jersey National Trust sign indicating **Le Don Mourant** and place name) you can look back and see Devil's Hole on the far side of this cove with its near vertical walls. As you round this promontory you can look across the next inlet, its ramparts riven with caves. On the far side, in turn, you can look back and view L'Ile Agois, a small island just detached from the mainland.

At the next promontory, marked by a bench seat, you must head inland by the track between fields, past **Crabbé Farm**. The

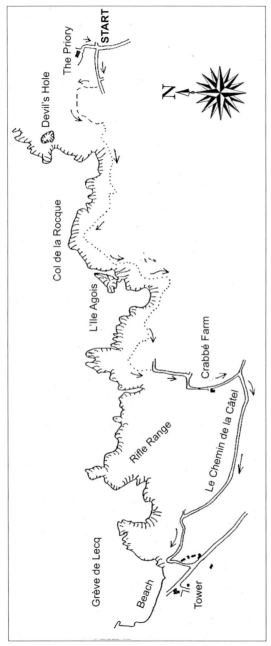

O.S. map shows the coast path continuing around the next finger of land – Rouge Nez – behind the **Rifle Range**. This route should NOT be attempted. The earth wall behind the target area has been heaped up and the seaward side is loose scree and is set above a sheer drop to the sea below. It is a great pity that this bit of the coast is a no go area for ramblers but it would be foolish to tackle it at present.

Head past the diminutive **Crabbé Farm** and turn right to follow the lane above Les Vaux de Lecq – this will lead you by a pleasant route until you descend to reach **Grève de Lecq** with all its facilities, including the bus. This section of the walk is described in Walk 29.

St. Mary's Parish is relatively small but includes one of the most spectacular portions of the North Coast Path – from the Mourier Valley to Grève de Lecq – which also seems to be one of the least frequented by walkers. Between the promontories of Le Col de la Rocque and Rouge Nez (near Crabbé), both of which provide fine viewing points, the path stays close to the cliff face and the experience is quite awe-inspiring. The relentless attack of the sea against the steep precipices has everywhere excavated caves. From the promontory between Col de la Rocque and L'Ane one can look eastwards across the inlet to L'Ile Agois, a tiny green-topped islet separated from the mainland by a steep, deep gorge. Much evidence of prehistoric man has been found here, as well as coins dating from the ninth century A.D.

L'Ile Agois

Grève de Lecq

GREVE DE LECQ CIRCULAR

via Les Vaux de Lecq, Le Rondin and Le Chemin du Catel

This walk includes a substantial stretch of permissive path – not a right of way, but a path through private land which walkers are permitted by the landowner to make use of. This offers a way along the edge of the hanging wood on the south side of the valley. The second leg of the walk is via a quiet lane, known as Le Chemin du Câtel, which offers an elevated view back across the valley and has always been a personal favourite.

Start:	Grève de Lecq
Map Reference:	583554
Bus:	Nos. 7B, 9 to Grève de Lecq
Parking:	Either of the two large car parks at Grève de Lecq
Distance:	4 kilometers

From Grève de Lecq, with your back to the sea, take the road on the right past the Martello tower and the car park which surrounds it. At the old property ahead on the left you leave the road by turning left along the unmade track which passes just to the right of the house. This is the start of the permissive path referred to above.

The path follows the edge of the wood, passing Le Moulin de Lecq, with its waterwheel intact and still turning, at least spasmodically. A little further along you can see a small reservoir, which captures the stream flowing along the valley bottom and, formerly, onto the sands at Grève de Lecq.

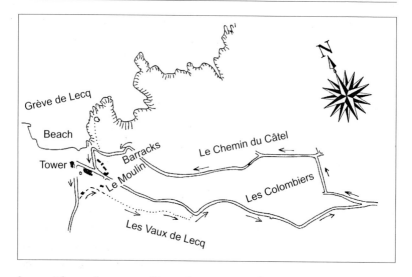

The path eventually ends at a gate where you bear left to join the road which connects Grève de Lecq with the village centre of St. Mary's. There is a sign indicating **Le Don Somers Clark** and space for one or two cars to pull in off the road.

Turn right and follow the road until you see the former **Rondin Motors**. Here you turn sharp left up the lane, past **Les Colombiers** and an unusually large field on the left to reach a T-junction. Turn left here to follow the lane known as **Le Chemin de Catel**. At the fork you bear left (the right fork takes you past Crabbé Farm and on to the cliff path to Devil's Hole). From this fork, the coast path has been diverted to follow Le Chemin as it descends to Grève de Lecq.

On the way you will pass the **Firing Range**. You look towards the impressive conical hill which stands sentinel on the east side of the bay. You may be tempted to explore the grassy track to the right which leads you to **Le Câtel Fort**, comprising a walled enclosure with a hut and three gun emplacements and all well maintained by the Jersey National Trust. Then follow the narrow lane down to Grève de Lecq, with all its facilities.

Grève de Lecq is without doubt the most developed spot on the north coast. There is easy access from two directions and the bay itself has a good sandy beach though it shelves steeply, especially at high water. The pubs, cafés, hotels and night clubs are not without their attractions. A visit to Le Moulin de Lecq is a must. It has its waterwheel intact and still working, and the gears are impressively displayed behind the bar. To see them suddenly lurch into motion, particularly after a pint or two of the excellent Guernsey bitter on sale here, is a sobering experience indeed!

Câtel de Lecq is the 270 foot high mound which guards the bay on its east side. This has been a fortified position since prehistoric times. The Câtel now belongs to the Jersey National Trust and access to it is signposted along the path leading off the narrow lane which ascends the hill behind the lower car park. There is a small enclosure and some gun emplacements positioned behind gaps in the wall – an unusual vantage point across the bay.

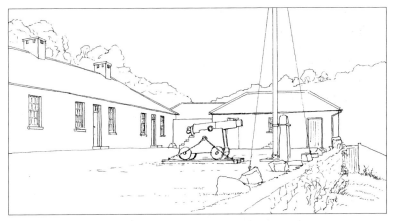

Grève de Lecq Barracks: The single-storey buildings on the hillside beside the lane were built in the early nineteenth century and used by the Jersey Militia and by British troops while stationed on the island, and were later utilised as private houses. Now restored by the Jersey National Trust, the buildings in part comprise a dwelling once again and contain a number of exhibits relating to their history.

GREVE DE LECQ - PLEMONT

This section of the North Coast Path digresses a little inland soon after leaving Grève de Lecq and is fairly up and down in its course to Plémont. Refreshments usually available at either end.

Start:	Grève de Lecq
Map Reference:	583554
Bus:	Nos.7B, 9 to Greve de Lecq, No.8 from Plémont
Parking:	Either of the large car parks at Grève de Lecq
Distance:	4 kilometres

With your back to the sea at Grève de Lecq, bear right towards the **Prince of Wales**. The start of the coast path is the drive immediately to the left of this large, modern pub. A fairly steep climb takes you past a few houses – once past the last of these be sure to look back for a fine view over Grève de Lecq and its little harbour. The path levels out to become a farm track and then a metalled lane.

Turn right at the farm buildings and follow the lane past Lecq Farm and along the gravel track beside the outbuildings, then sharp left by a footpath which descends beside a field. The path crosses the stream by a plank bridge and ascends the far side. A waterfall descends the cliff face at the last inlet before the small beach known as Le Petit Plémont. Now follow the coast path towards the headland, almost separated from the mainland, known as La Tête de Plémont.

The unlovely buildings of the former Plémont Holiday Camp face the coast path. At the time of writing, this site awaits redevelopment. A detour is possible just past here, by way of the path which branches off to the right and leads down to La Tête

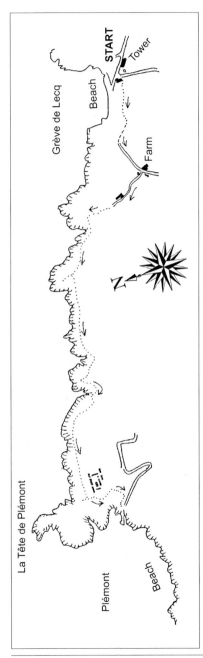

de Plémont. You can continue along the coast path to reach the bus stop and car park or bear right along the metalled path to reach the café above Plémont and thence by steps down to the beach (tide permitting).

Other Channel Islands: All along the north coast, providing the weather is not too murky, you will have spotted a number of other islands and reefs. From east to west these include the Ecréhous (see Walk 7), the Dirouilles (rocky reef), Alderney in the far distance, the Paternosters (Walk 26), and the islands of Sark, Herm, Jethou and Guernsey.

Alderney is the most remote of all the islands but the closest to France and is only visible on the clearest days. Sark's awesome cliffs rise dramatically from the sea directly north of Jersey; this island was first settled by Jersey folk in the fifteenth century and Jersey names are still common there. Herm is lower-lying and the uncompromising hump of Jethou is just to the west. Guernsey is the long, gently inclined land mass to the north-west.

German tower, near Gros Nez

PLEMONT - L'ETACQ

This last leg of the North Coast Path is its most level section, without great climbs in and out of bays. The ruins of Grosnez Castle mark the half way point at Jersey's north-westerly corner. The coast path from Grosnez to L'Etacq is probably the bleakest and most windswept bit of the island – even the gorse submits to the blast and spreads across the ground like ivy rather than standing up in bushes. There are usually opportunities for refreshment at either end.

Start: Bus terminus/car park at Plémont
Map Reference: 563564
Bus: No.8 to Plémont; No.12A from L'Etacq
Parking: Parking beside road leading down to Plémont or at bus terminus on cliff top
Distance: 5 Kilometres

From the bus stop and car park above Plémont the cliff path westwards is found on the far side of the track leading down to the Bay. Simply follow the path above the cliffs, first above Plémont and then over rocky headlands until you reach Grosnez, with its views north towards the other Channel Islands.

The granite cliffs around here are the favoured haunt of Jersey's rock climbers.

The great headland south of Grosnez is known as Les Landes and is a common where you are free to wander. A little inland you will see the boundary fence of the Race Course. Not surprisingly, the Germans fortified this strategic corner of the island with Teutonic thoroughness. I suggest the most rewarding route here is to stick to the coast path as it passes gun emplacement

The graveyard of the guns

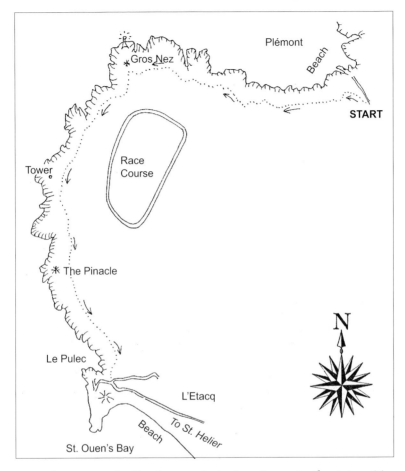

and tower and affords a perfect view down to the totem-like
Pinnacle Rock with the remains of its prehistoric settlements
clearly visible. At the bottom of the cliff, just south of the German
tower, is a large number of heavy calibre artillery weapons, visible
at low tide. These are guns of mixed origin, some believed to be
Russian, captured by the Germans in World War II and installed
by them on the island for coastal defence during the Occupation.
At the end of the war the British liberating forces threw them
over the cliffs. One has subsequently been retrieved and set up at
Noirmont – see Walk 16.

Le Pinacle from the north

The granite formations in the vicinity are spectacular and the shape of the rocks and the jointing is very similar to the granite of Land's End in Cornwall or to the rocks of the Côte de Granit Rose in Brittany.

The path begins to descend towards the road but you will surely wish to pause to take in the magnificent southward curve of St. Ouen's Bay ending in the exclamation mark of Corbière lighthouse – one of Jersey's great views.

Follow the main road passing the slipway to the little inlet Le Pulec – on the right and bear left to the bus stop at this northerly point of St. Ouen's Bay, and the end of the North Coast Path.

The coastal path crossing boggy ground

Plémont is a beautiful bay with a character of its own, but not accessible at high tide when the sea covers the entire beach. Otherwise there is a fine expanse of hard sand, lots of smooth granite rocks and clear rock pools. The bay is backed by spectacular cliffs with caves everywhere. It is all most dramatic and children especially will love exploring here (but beware the rising tide). The bay is called La Grève au Lanchon, 'Lanchon' referring to the sand eels which are here prevalent – look out for them in the rock pools left when the tide ebbs.

Grosnez Castle

Grosnez comprises the north-west corner of the island and is the point where the north coast path turns south to L'Etacq at the head of St. Ouen's Bay. Here are the somewhat scanty remains of a castle which relied for defence mainly upon the precipitous cliffs which surround it on three sides. The arch was part of the gatehouse and defended by a moat and battlemented walls with slits through which archers could launch their arrows. The origin of Grosnez Castle is obscure but the visible evidence suggests a date around the fourteenth or fifteenth centuries and that it deteriorated through age rather than being destroyed in battle.

Afterword

Although I was already well acquainted with almost all the routes described, for the purpose of compiling this book I walked them all at least once, and usually more than once, during four equally spaced visits to the island – in February, May, August and November. It actually snowed in February and conditions on the North Coast Path, where I guess the wind chill factor was at least minus 10, were almost too awful to enjoy the walking. I must say it was a joy to find the bar of the Bouley Bay Hotel open in such adverse conditions. In May Jersey was covered in flowers, including a bumper crop of white campion; in August it was hot and sunny and swimming could be mixed freely with walking. In November the land was stripped bare and the views seemed incredibly clear and well defined. Walking in Jersey is a joy at any time, but extreme heat and cold are best avoided, thus making spring and autumn ideal seasons.

There are so many bits of Jersey that I long to explore by public footpath, if only those ways existed. There is no doubt that the States have done a great service in opening up the coastal paths and various short stretches inland, often in cooperation with the Jersey National Trust and other landowners. Since the first edition of this book, in 1992, many more stretches of footpath have been opened up, including the coast path from Beauport to Corbière (see Walk 13), a number of worthwhile bits in St. Peter (see Walk 18) and the very enjoyable Sentier des Moulins (see Walk 19). At the time of writing, the States seem intent on enlarging the Island's network of footpaths, and more power to their elbow. The Green Lane system is a welcome development, but walking along metalled lanes, which are still open to motor vehicles, is no sustitute for the genuine footpath experience.

I dream of footpaths along all the valleys, so that one might cross the island from one coast path to another, and of the completion of the coast path itself from St. Aubin to Noirmont, and from Fliquet to Rozel. And would not a path along the edge of the plateau facing St. Ouen's Bay provide a superb walk – somewhere above La Rue de la Mare. And what about reinstating all those ancient sanctuary paths, from parish churches to the coast? One can but dream.

Above: The Railway Walk (see Walk 17)

Below: An old Jersey tractor

The *Jersey Collection* from SEAFLOWER BOOKS

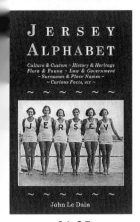

£4.95

£9.95

£5.95

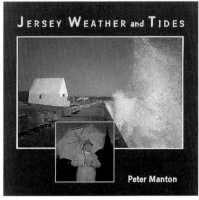

£6.95

£5.95

£6.95

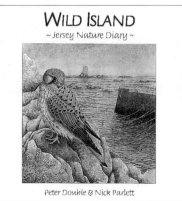

£5.95

£7.95

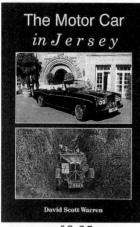